Going Somewhere

A Continuing Journey into Honest Horsemanship

Going Somewhere

A Continuing Journey into Honest Horsemanship

Tom Moates

Copyright © 2013 by Tom Moates

ALL RIGHTS RESERVED. No part of this book may be reproduced or transmitted in any form by any means, electronic or mechanical, including photocopying and recording, or by any information storage and retrieval system, except as may be expressly permitted in writing from the publisher. Requests for permission should be addressed to Spinning Sevens Press, Attn: Rights and Permissions, P.O. Box 440 Floyd, Virginia, 24091.

ISBN 978-0-9845850-5-2

Designed by Chris Legg

Cover photo by Louise Ellingsworth, Bob Grave, Alex Mufson, Jan Murphy, and Melissa Pelletier.

Cover image enhancements by Nancy Lawson, www.SageCanyonStudio.com

Special thanks to cover models Beau and HZ

Dedication

This book is dedicated to my good friend and neighbor, Derrick Hicks.

It's well earned, for without Derrick's trustworthiness, capability, and willingness to be on-call to watch over my farm and horses while I'm away, most of my travels to clinics wouldn't have happened, and this book (and most of the others) simply wouldn't exist.

It's also my pleasure to dedicate this book to him—I've yet to meet a man who more personifies the Golden Rule. We spend hours working horses together. He generously lets me tag along with one of the Big-Uns when he's got cattle to check. He's right there offering panels, truck, trailer, and a strong back when it's time to set up for the annual Bible/horsemanship clinic we host each fall. And that's not the half of it....

So for all this and much more, *Going Somewhere* is rightly dedicated to you, Derrick!

Other Books by Tom Moates:

Discovering Natural Horsemanship
Round-Up: A Gathering of Equine Writings

(The Honest Horsemanship Series:)
A Horse's Thought
Between the Reins
Further Along the Trail

Contents

Foreword .... *i*
Acknowledgments .... *v*
Introduction .... *vii*

Chapter 1   Ideal Versus Adverse Conditions, Part One:
            The Wreck! 1
Chapter 2   Ideal Versus Adverse Conditions, Part Two:
            Thinking About it 13
Chapter 3   Mister Dinky the Mule
            (The Dinky Chronicles, Part One) 27
Chapter 4   Free Searching with Sunshine in Montana 41
Chapter 5   Trailer Loading Mirage 53
Chapter 6   Dinky Days (The Dinky Chronicles, Part Two) 67
Chapter 7   Harry's Definition of Training: The Rest of
            the Story 79
Chapter 8   Hey, Everybody! 85
Chapter 9   Travels with Harry 93
Chapter 10 Flagging Dinky (The Dinky Chronicles,
            Part Three) 117
Afterword   139

(Pam Talley Stoneburner)

Foreword

    5:00 p.m. sharp the phone rings and it's Tom. I say, "Hello," and he asks, "Has there been any 'foreword' progress?"

    You see, this latest book was done except the Foreword, which means the project was on hold until I wrote it. I don't think writers—I mean true writers—understand the stress and anguish a non-writer goes through when trying to write. It's a simple foreword, they say. It can be short. Just arrange a few words, etc., etc.

No, they don't get it.

Tom is a writer. Nowhere in my life will you find notes I've written from something I've attended, whereas Tom has notes, notes, and more notes. He can't help himself. He must write his thoughts down on paper. It doesn't matter if it's at a clinic, traveling with me, or after a day of helping others with their horses, Tom writes about it.

But we're glad he does. By writing down those thoughts he has an accurate record of what took place, places, people, horses, times, and feelings all recorded to share with us. By writing it down Tom reinforces it in his own mind and can go back to compare, draw conclusions, see similar results, etc., all of which makes better reading for us.

We can share in his experience with horses and life. We can empathize with the frustration. And we can laugh with the truth of real life. All in all it makes for a good read. But that doesn't make my job any easier. However, here I sit pen in hand, and having read this latest book, here's a few thoughts.

I see growth in Tom's horsemanship evidenced in his writing. Tom's writing, I think, comes partly from his generosity. If he understands something he must share it, and writing is one way to do that. Another way is helping people with horses, or mules—you'll enjoy reading about a mule named Dinky. Tom keeps helping more people; what a wonderful way to grow in your knowledge of anything is to teach it, but with that experience is more knowledge to write about, and so he does.

During Tom's travels with me he would be writing long after I was in bed asleep. Thus in the chapter of "Travels with Harry" I felt worn out and tired after he recalls all we did in one day. I couldn't have recalled it all, but it's written down in Tom's little notebook.

People seem to get a lot out of Tom's other books. So out of Tom's notes comes another book, both enjoyable and thought provoking. They are stores of Tom's experiences, but most have a lesson for us to contemplate. So from this non-writer I say, thank you Tom for writing. Don't weaken—we're looking "foreword" to more!

Harry Whitney
April 2013

Acknowledgments

An enormous amount of appreciation goes to Harry Whitney. I'm glad for the time he spends logging the miles and the years teaching these clinics and that I'm able to be a part of it. I'd like to give him a very special thanks for letting me tag along in the RV with him across six states, some of which is recounted in this book. Finally, I'd like to express my deepest gratitude to him for sharing his gift of a very special kind of horsemanship with us folks who are in awe of it and want to grasp as much of it as we possibly can! Thanks again, Harry!

I'm delighted Kelly Robinson, veteran book editor from my past several titles, returned as the editor for this book. Her care and expertise with the manuscript provides such a peace of mind for this writer—it's a comfort to be in such professional hands. Thank you again, Kelly!

Chris Legg again put the mark of his graphic design genius on this new book and designed the cover. He keeps the feel between the titles in this series consistent, and his many hours of devoted work are greatly appreciated.

A tremendous thanks goes to all the photographers who helped tell these stories by generously allowing me to use their images: Jan Bellin, Bob Grave, Michéle Jedlicka, Dianne Madden, Carol Moates, Pam Talley Stoneburner, and Harry Whitney. And to all the photographers from the cover photo shoot (whether or not their image actually is the one used), I appreciate each one for getting up early and manning a camera in the Arizona desert: Louise Ellingsworth, Bob Grave, Alex Mufson, Melissa Pelletier, and Jan Murphy. Also, a huge thanks to Louise Ellingsworth and Jan Murphy for letting Harry and me ride their horses, HZ and Beau, for the photo shoot.

A big thanks to Nancy Lawson of www.SageCanyonStudio.com for putting her great talents to work and providing some enhancements to the cover image.

Carol Moates deserves a special thanks. Being married to this writer means she puts up with me while working on these books. It also mean she puts in extra hours as a consultant—I'm forever bouncing ideas, photos, chapter drafts, and tons of other things off her. (She tolerates it fairly well.) Her input is greatly appreciated!

(Alex Mufson)

Introduction

Horsemanship clinician, Harry Whitney, and I were discussing this book one evening during a clinic at his place in Salome, Arizona. It was late February 2013 and the book was coming along nicely. Already I was thinking about the cover and knew in a matter of weeks we'd be putting it together.

By strokes of luck, when it was time to design the covers for

Harry Whitney begins work on getting Jan Murphy' horse, Beau, to bow at a clinic in Salome, Arizona in March 2013. *(Tom Moates)*

the previous three books in this series, the right cover photographs were already in-hand. The series is sometimes called the "Honest Horsemanship Series" due to the running subtitle, *A Continuing Journey into Honest Horsemanship*—the first book in the series is, *A Horse's Thought*, followed by *Between the Reins* and then *Further Along the Trail*. For this latest one, no such perfect cover photo existed. Time was running out to find the right image, so I started to think specifically about what I'd want in a picture, and to see if I might set it up.

"I've been thinking about the new book's cover," I told Harry, "and I'd like to have you and me riding a couple of horses. I think I'd like our backs to the camera like we're going somewhere."

"That's it!" he said.

"That's what?" I asked.

"Your title—*Going Somewhere*." [Another dilemma I still had to sort out was what to call the new book.]

And so, Harry was right!

The books are a series of memoirs about my progress working with horses in a way that strives to get the horse to be willing and feel positive about working with the person—and to "See things from the horse's point of view," as Harry is noted for saying. I sincerely hope I am *Going Somewhere* because I know I can improve my horsemanship and get to deeper levels of understanding with these amazing creatures if I keep at it. One of the new places I've gotten to, which is reflected in this book, is working more with other people and their horses.

Over a year ago I officially began hiring out here locally to help folks one-on-one with their horses. The truth is, working as a trainer is a role I never envisioned myself undertaking.

Anyone familiar with my previous books likely understands when I say that the image I carried of myself was one of a perpetual student of the horse and of Harry. I'm usually the one trying to figure stuff out, after all. Perhaps I'll venture a little further and say that with my obsession to write about the incredible and nebulous realm of horsemanship, I've seen myself as more of a scribe. The thought of taking on the role of straight-up teaching horsemanship just never crossed my mind.

Slowly, however, over time, I realized the horsemanship I'd been learning from Harry often filled my cup, spilled over, and sloshed around here locally. It began with a little conversation here. Then, getting friends to a Harry clinic there. Then, a few folks asking me to come work with a horse or two. The next thing I knew, I was heading out several times a week to work with other folks and their horses and really benefitting from the experiences.

Unfamiliar horses fascinate me and there's little I enjoy more than observing their behavior and seeing what I can do with them. I love to play around and discover who each horse is and how I can shape up this or that with how they interact with a person. I'm hopelessly obsessed with this. In retrospect, it seems pretty clear that I might be well suited to help some folks with their horses; it's just a destination I never intentionally aimed for.

The fit was, however, perfect—I got to work with a wider range of horses to help me grow in my horsemanship and other folks seemed to get something out of it. Plus, I've also gained new material from these experiences for some chapters. Talk about a win, win, win....

Initially, one of my anxieties was wondering whether or not I could put into words what I thought people needed to do to get a positive change with their horses. It is one thing for me to work with a horse and get things going better—it is something altogether different to help another person grasp ideas that they can use to get improvements. This has gone better than I expected.

Perhaps sitting at the keyboard for years and working hard to express many of these same ideas in written form translates well into speaking with people during a session. Not only can I pull from a list of understandings based on what Harry teaches, but I also have tons of phrases, metaphors, and anecdotes (some of my own and some borrowed from Harry or from others at his clinics) at the ready to help explain things to others as they unfold in real time when working horses.

I quoted Harry in *A Horse's Thought* in the chapter called, "Pushing the Envelope," saying, "In our comfort, there's no room for growth." Specifically, in that instance, it was a reference to people working with horses. Yet, the same applies here to my training work. And, as uncomfortable as it has been to venture out into the wilderness of helping strangers and unfamiliar horses, it has been incredibly rewarding.

In a short time I have been hands-on with a wider variety of horses and horse issues than ever before. Sometimes I see some things right away to suggest for improvements. At other times, it is challenging to find a point that combines what I see going on with a horse and where I think a person might grasp a suggestion to get real and lasting traction towards a better relationship with the horse. The result for me is a level of growth in my own horsemanship I wouldn't

Tom riding Festus (The Bestest) in the round pen during the September 2012 Bible/horsemanship clinic in Floyd, Virginia. (*Carol Moates*)

have seen so quickly otherwise.

I love working with the Big-Uns (Jubal [The Wonder Horse] and Festus [The Bestest]), and all the other usual suspects here, but we have spent so much time together that when working with them now my growth seems quite linear. Sometimes that line points up, sometimes it points down, but the work feels like it's usually along the same lines. Put another way, we have the same issues to tackle each time we go to work. In fact, sometimes it feels like we're not getting anywhere at all.

Perhaps we just know each other too well and my creativity to come up with new alternative methods to improve our togetherness dulls from time to time. Shaking up that status quo by working with a variety of new horses really helps me come back home, putting to use fresh approaches to help my Big-Uns and notice where the lack of clarity between us is evident. Also, a momentum builds from working the new horses and it continues to roll when I get back home. It's much like going to a clinic, which always gets things stirred up in my head and seems to reinvigorate my horse work with my guys.

So, back to the clinic in Salome and the cover photo. I knew that clinic would be the one window of opportunity for a cover shot of the two of us riding together. Harry said he'd be up for it but, as is so often the case, time slips away from us. Friday night came, the clinic was finished, and Harry and I would need to leave his place at 8:30 the next morning for me to be in Phoenix on time to catch my flight back home.

Several folks were staying through the weekend and for the next week of clinic, too. I asked two riders from the week, Louise Ellingsworth and Jan Murphy, if they'd be willing to saddle up their horses for a few minutes very early the next morning for a photo shoot. They were happy to do it. Harry already had turned in for the night by this time.

What a bunch of great sports these folks were! At dawn the next morning HZ (a.k.a. Hey Zeus), Louise's horse, and Beau, Jan's

Harry and Tom riding HZ and Beau in the desert during the quick morning photo shoot in Salome, Arizona. (*Alex Mufson*)

horse, were saddled up and ready to go. Harry emerged from his RV. Alex Mufson, Bob Grave, and Melissa Pelletier also were one hand. Harry hopped on HZ and I climbed aboard Beau, and with the sun now up we rode up the driveway and around the desert with the other five all snapping photos.

It was awesome! I can't thank my friends enough for helping to pull off that photo shoot on such short notice and with so little time that morning to work with.

Which brings me to conclude this Introduction so you can go get started reading the new book! I just want to add that the friendships and acquaintances I've gained from attending Harry's clinics are very special to me. So much of what I've learned about horsemanship has come from watching others ride at clinics. I'm very fortunate to have seen many serious students work with their horses while Harry coached them. Then, watching Harry ride is, well...an education in itself and a goal to shoot for. If you ever have a chance to ride a horse right after Harry has been on it, you'll experience an education in feel, as well! And finally, the great questions put forth by the inquisitive students to Harry at the discussion tables over the years have done as much to further my own horsemanship as my own ten million questions.

    I hope you enjoy reading this new leg of my journey and that your own horsemanship is *Going Somewhere* great!

Chapter 1

(Pam Talley Stoneburner)

Ideal Versus Adverse Conditions, Part One: The Wreck!

There wasn't even time to yell, "Jubal!" as I slumped out of the saddle and collapsed in a heap on the ground.

And just when my experiment was shaping up...!

It all started a half hour earlier. Carol and I were heading home in the car along a stretch of gravel road up the hill from where I now lay. We had noticed that our neighbors' cows were out. I went home and called Derrick Hicks, who owns the cattle with his brother, Jeffrey, and father, David.

Jubal (The Wonder Horse) could be pretty good or really horrid when ridden out, with or without other horses along. Getting the gelding "with me" from the start and keeping that with-you-ness when heading out to ride somewhere was a huge challenge. With-you-ness is a cornerstone of all that I've learned about horses from Harry over the years. It is a phrase he coined and defined which debuted in a chapter back in the very first book of this series, *A Horse's Thought*.

I'd been working for a long time to get Jubal to feel better and be okay in such scenarios. In fact, Harry rode Jubal as his saddle horse for five weeks of clinics at Mendin' Fences Farm in Tennessee in 2010. Afterward, he had discussed with me that he could feel Jubal's tendency to mentally wander into nasty territory when heading out onto a trail ride. He explained that I'd need to be on my toes to keep ahead of trouble by diligently keeping Jubal with-me from the very start of a ride out into the great beyond. The big gelding and I had experienced varying degrees of success with this in the years since then. Perhaps it's more accurate to admit that I had been able to apply myself to this task to varying degrees, thus the range of results. A couple of the better times had been when we fetched a stray cow or two for our neighbors.

Even earnest attempts to keep Jubal's thoughts with me and then carrying that togetherness out of the pasture and down the road, inevitably failed at some point along the way. I'd lose my touch and not be able to stay ahead of him. Once I missed it, the gelding usually melted down into a bundle of nerves, barely holding it together at times. I'd have no luck getting big enough to get him to really let go of those spastic, worried thoughts.

I realized this is where I was falling short in supporting him. I felt like I ought to be able to get bigger out there so he could let go of all that stuff and feel better about following along with me. To my credit, I could manage to hang in there (sometimes doing some groundwork for awhile) and get some improvement before turning back in the direction of home. But I just couldn't quite get it done. It seemed elusive to me to get him clearly between the reins out there in the moment, where he could let the baggage go and just be okay with me in that place.

Ultimately, Jubal would not be able to settle down in earnest until I got headed back and nearly home with him. I was frustrated because I knew I could improve my presentation and persistence and get some of this worked out better but kept falling short of the mark.

So, back to the situation with the cows. Carol and I pulled up to our house just having seen the rogue cattle. I thought, "Here is a great job to experiment with! I'll throw my saddle in the truck and grab Jubal out of the pasture and let him run along side the truck on a halter down to the neighbor's place."

I knew he'd be worried to some extent. I figured to saddle him down there, do a little ground work to get him as with me as I could, and then mount up to see if I might get him lining out on a job gathering those cows. The big hope was that I'd be capable of getting him more with me as the ride went along.

The initial phases of this experiment went worse than expected. Jubal was really unglued and just quivering before we ever reached the farm next door. Already it occurred to me that if we'd begun with some groundwork, then gone up the road a ways and then back, and so on, that things might at least have been better for him at the start. But the call of a real job was strong on my mind. I didn't have all day to prepare Jubal if I was going to use him to get these cows gathered and back across the road. And honestly, so much ground needed to be covered—some steep and wooded—a horse was perfect for the task and I had several of them I longed to be able to use for just such a purpose. Plus, I really wanted to see if I

Derrick Hick works with Whisky, a Quarter Horse owned by his brother Jeffrey, at the 2012 Floyd, Virginia Bible/horsemanship clinic.
(*Carol Moates*)

could get him improving along the way in such a situation.

There was an old cinderblock milk house that had a little grassy area and some board fence in front where I stopped the truck. I stepped out, lead rope still in hand, and commenced to doing some groundwork with Jubal. I worked to block those troubling thoughts and get him with me. It didn't go very well. By this point I was well aware that I had us deep into Adverse Conditions Territory. (Call it ACT and it sounds like a disorder, doesn't it?) I considered the options and decided to forge ahead and see if we could get a job done that needed doing right then and get improvement along the way.

Jubal, usually good to stand while I got in the saddle, was so gone even this was a challenge. I worked and worked on getting his thought and settling him there. I did manage to get a leg over him without him prancing off. Then I lined him out across a hayfield towards an open gate that needed to be closed. We got there and I dismounted and chained it shut. I worked him again from the ground and then remounted.

Next, we needed to cross the hay field, which happened to be in the direction of home, and then go through an open gate at the far end and close it behind us before doubling back and heading after the cows. I kept checking in with Jubal—stopping and backing him when he'd start to get away from me mentally, which was constantly. He did begin to settle down a little, though. When we reached the gate, I deliberately rode beyond it and trotted some circles in the hayfield. Things definitely started to improve.

In the circles, I'd let off a little forward pressure on the side heading away from home and turn up the heat just a bit on the arc that headed for home. His head eventually came down some, and I'd let him go straight a few strides when it did and then circle again. A conversation was happening

Tom works on establishing some with-you-ness with Jubal before saddling up. *(Pam Talley Stoneburner)*

between us finally. A little more stopping, backing, circling and such and I actually had Jubal's thoughts breaking away from elsewhere and occasionally coming more along the lines I was presenting. It was far from great but to be so far out there into Adverse Conditions Territory it went much better than many previous efforts. Even I relaxed just a tad at this point.

When things were pretty decent (relatively) I rode through the gate, dismounted, closed it, and remounted. The big gelding was far from relaxed, though. The tension was palpable, and although things were getting better than expected considering the very unsettled start we'd had, Jubal still felt like a brick.

We trotted along a section of old woven wire fence and I had him on my line (the course I was projecting out from for us to take) fairly well. The brush had consumed some of that fence. The occasional tree shot skyward from between two posts and branched out way above the wire and weeds. The fence separated a pasture from the hay field we had just crossed. We were on the pasture side at present and the breeze had grass and branches fluttering everywhere.

We jogged along a line intended to circle behind about 30 head of wayward cattle now visible in a valley a little ways off. I was plenty excited to have a horse of mine out in the world on a real job, and we were just about to make contact with the cattle. The valley sloped downhill and then fell off sharply to a wooded mountainside that dropped all the way to a river. I hoped to fall in behind the cows and get them moving uphill towards a gate that led back across the road into their proper pasture. My unfortunate circumstance occurred then, even before we got close to the first cow.

My best guess is a Tufted Titmouse flew out of the brush along the fence and spooked my massive, roundish, sorrel companion. Quite deftly, The Wonder Horse took an unannounced, unwanted, but very athletic lateral step away from the booger.

Jubal's flinchy hop wasn't much, really—just the smallest spooked scootch sideways as we went along. Honestly, I wouldn't have come out of the saddle if, when I reflexively braced my left leg against the stirrup to counter his sudden move, my lower back hadn't made a nasty *crack!*

I remember thinking, "Should I stay aboard? Oh no...something snapped, better just...."

Thud!

Experiencing the simultaneous sound and vibration of that sudden spinal adjustment caused me some worry. I've endured a bad lower back for two decades, so I know when it goes out. There was no doubt about it, in that instant it went way out. That stupid crack, however, was a new twist. I'd never heard or felt that before. I cleared my booted feet from the stirrups and let myself just go with gravity over to my left and onto the ground.

I lay there on my side for a second not sure what that crack meant and wondered if I could move my toes. Then I worried about Jubal and what he was doing. I tilted my head and looked. There stood The Wonder Horse right beside me, maybe one step beyond where I took the plunge, head down grazing away in his brindle.

"Jubal!" I finally managed. He ignored me.

I rolled onto my back and noticed the puffy white clouds passing above at a quick clip. How picturesque viewed from this unusual vantage point, I thought. I wiggled my toes...ah, good sign!

Munch, munch, munch.

"Jubal!"

I pushed myself over and managed to crouch on my knees. Already the misaligned muscles were twisting my midsection; I could feel it. I reached over, grabbed a split rein off the ground, and shook it.

"Jubal! Stop grazing in that bridle!"

Reaching up with the other hand I gripped a stirrup and pulled myself up. This bout with my back was a bad one, oh boy.

I hugged my trusty horse around the neck—"Jubal! Stop eating that grass!" I pulled the cell phone from the holder on my belt and called Carol. I told her what happened and got her on the way with ibuprofen and water. With Jubal as my hungry crutch, we walked very, very slowly getting back on track behind the straggling half herd that still remained in the valley—"Stop it, Jubal! Get that head up here! Can't you see I'm in pain!" He took full advantage of my compromised condition to grab every mouthful he could while I was at a big disadvantage to get him to leave that thought. Even so, we eventually got in behind the bovine escapees and herded them towards their home.

I wasn't the only one hobbling around out there at that moment, although I was supposed to be the non-crippled-up one. My friend, Derrick, was up on the road and wore a big brace from his crotch to the calf on one leg. He had undergone surgery for a torn ACL ligament a few weeks earlier. Derrick works as a logger, and a Maple limb he cut that was under pressure snapped around and whacked him in the leg tearing the ligament

Derrick on his Quarter Horse colt, Punkin' Head, and Tom on Derrick's twenty-something Appaloosa gelding, Comanche, on a Sunday afternoon working horses in Derrick's round pen. *(Carol Moates)*

loose from the bone. With me doubled over and gnarled up sideways leaning on Jubal, barely able to look ahead to where we were walking, and Derrick doing a Hopalong Cassidy routine ushering cattle across the road back into their proper pasture, we were a pretty pitiful sight. We did, however, get the job done!

The end of this long story is that Carol (armed with added ammunition from our family doctor, whom she had called) insisted I go to the emergency room about an hour away and really get my back checked out this time. Had it not been for the back crack in the saddle I wouldn't have been so easily convinced. But I must admit, the involuntary "chiropractic adjustment" had my curiosity roused with this one. I half expected to have x-rays taken and the doctor come back and say, "Man, how have you been walking around for the past 15 years?"

The results were less dramatic. Actually, everything on the x-rays looked fine, just some typical aging stuff going on (oh, well!). It seems that I simply suffer from a weak area of musculature in my lower back and when I tweak it, the subsequent spasms send my body into a misshapen mess for a week. The doctor sent me on my way with an additional back strengthening exercise to add to the ones I already do. It has helped, so I guess the amount of money (!) the insurance and I spent on that visit wasn't a total waste.

Clearly that's not the horse point here, though. I'll have to go way back to the very beginning of the story (when I still could walk upright) to pick that thread back up. Suffice it to say, quite a bit led up to the Tufted Titmouse incident, all of which involved decisions I made with Jubal, a horse I know as well as any in the world. But I wanted to start right off at the point of the wreck because it is an excellent illustration of where one can end up when venturing into Adverse Conditions Territory with an unprepared, un-with-you horse, even one as amazing and über-experienced as Jubal. I'll get to the "unprepared" part in a minute, but for now let's just start another chapter and begin with two key definitions....

Chapter 2

(Pam Talley Stoneburner)

Ideal Versus Adverse Conditions, Part Two: Thinking About It

Ideal conditions—a round corral or arena with level sandy footing (moistened with a light sprinkling of water to hinder the dust), tall panels that have the square corners that meet tightly together to deter a wayward hoof from getting caught, the temperature at a steady 74.5 degrees, sunny with a slight breeze, and Harry Whitney sitting just the other side of the fence with a fresh battery in his mobile microphone to answer any questions and provide insights while you ride.

Adverse conditions—hmm...(where to start?), anywhere that is 50 steps away from wherever a horse usually lives, being 20 steps away from any horse buddy, anywhere around wildlife, going after a neighbor's escaped cattle, rainy weather, windy weather, cold weather, hot weather, anywhere within sight of a trampoline with a kid on it, and anytime there is a real life reason to ask something of a horse right now because it really needs to happen.

Lately at clinics I've heard Harry discuss the contrast of working horses in ideal versus adverse conditions. I'm not sure if he recently began speaking about this or if he's talked about it over the years and it just finally sank into my brain. Maybe it was that trip to the emergency room I shared in the last chapter that made the idea hit home.

Regardless, Harry's point is simple—if a person doesn't have things going well with a horse under ideal conditions how can he possibly hope to have them working under adverse conditions?

It's rhetorical; one can't. (Not even on Jubal!)

Simply, Harry stresses that folks ought to do all they can to improve the relationship and communication with their horses in ideal settings to prepare their horses and themselves for forays into more adverse situations.

Perhaps this idea is better stated more emphatically (and using the pronoun "we" to secretly indicate that I really mean "me"). If we can't get our horses going in a soft, relaxed, willing way in ideal conditions then we won't have safe, effective results out under adverse circumstances. Or, restated yet again, if the horse can't be brought to a condition of with-you-ness in a classroom setting where very little external pressure exists, he's going to do anything but seek our input outside the gate when many more "real world" options and anxieties assault him.

Therefore, it is critical to develop the skills to get horses feeling better about things with humans through all the little opportunities that can be tinkered with at home. From haltering and saddling to groundwork and riding around the yard, find and work through any little spots of resistance and worry you can discover where their thoughts leave you. Try to see where the horse's attention drifts exactly when it happens and deal with it right away before it escalates even one more moment. Only then can we root out the origins of worries and other wayward thoughts, so sidetracks won't amplify and become huge problems when push comes to shove.

Sure, it is possible for horses to be brought along to a better condition of with-you-ness during a ride in the real world if the rider is, say, Harry. But if the rider is incapable of getting more with-you-ness with a particular horse in ideal settings, then that person very likely lacks the skills to get things going better with that horse during a ride "out there."

Of course, I've had to try it a bunch of times, so I've got some great supporting data on this hypothesis. Then there can be a situation like with Jubal in the last chapter where I actually was

Left-to-right, Ronnie Moyer, Sam Atnip, and Tom work moving cattle on a ranch in Colorado in late November, 2011—these experienced ranch horses are solid even in the adverse conditions of pastures and pens among cattle.
(Carol Moates)

getting things improving along the course of a ride while in adverse circumstances but not nearly enough to defuse Jubal's anxiety and keep us out of trouble. I also know there are horses Harry would not consider riding into adverse settings to work on until they had been brought further along in the more ideal spaces. I've witnessed this, too, and it is nice to know when to make that call—I'm guessing Jubal would have been in that category when I chose to head out with him that day.

Whether we're in the round pen or on the trail, if we are important and trustworthy enough to the horse to direct his thought, that is a real experience to him wherever he is. He doesn't differentiate between real and imaginary scenarios. They're all bona fide to him. If you are important and clear enough to the horse to get his attention and lead his thought in a round pen, that's it!

It takes a little imagination on the part of the human to bring a genuine "job" or "line to follow" into the ideal setting. ("Riding a line" is an idea Harry uses to discuss how the rider can project a path for the horse to follow—a whole chapter is devoted to this in the first book of the series, *A Horse's Thought*.) However, if our intentions are clearly presented, the horse picks up on them in either ideal or adverse settings. So, riding a line or doing a job can be done on the trail outside the fence from his buddies, as well as inside the round pen or arena.

On one hand, put some people in a round pen with a horse and often the lack of real world stuff going on can produce an insular environment. A bunch of sand and a dozen panels can seem boring to a person. One needs to brainstorm something to do which instigates a sense of importance in the person for the horse to pick up on. On the other hand, the difference when outside in the big world is that Tufted Titmice do lurk out there. They (I'll keep picking on the local birds, but it could be anything from litter to tractor trailers) create real issues to bother the horse and compete for that attention which the human is trying to gain and guide.

In an open spot like where Jubal and I were, the horse certainly has a wide range of things to deal with—missing the safety of his herd buddies, an unfamiliar environment, the rider also dealing with what's going on, cattle, etc. In such Adverse Conditions Territory it may not take much for the perceived danger of a potential booger to become much bigger than the rider to the horse. The horse then reacts (we might think of it as over-reacting) to take care of his own hide and the human gets mentally overridden and tuned out.

Harry tells a great story to help people understand how a Tufted Titmouse can move a 1200+ pound Jubal and send his rider to the hospital. The tale is a cult classic among Harry's students widely referred to as, "The Table Story." I'll recreate its mystery and intrigue to the best of my ability here.

It's a dark and stormy night. You're home alone in a big, old, creaky house. Lightning flashes, thunder reverberates, and driving rain pounds the window panes. The phone rings. You answer it, but there's just silence on the other end. "Hello?" you say. You hear breathing, and then click, the line goes dead—not even a dial tone. Hmm, that's weird, you think.

Then the power goes out. You're left in total darkness except for the occasional flashes of lightning which cast eerie shadows around the rooms before plunging you into total darkness again. You find a flashlight and go into the basement to check the fuse box. No help there, it's the outside line. There are noises on the floor above, so you cautiously climb back up the stairs and peer with your narrow flashlight beam around the living room. Tree limbs now are blowing against a window making tapping and scraping noises. The phone rings again. You answer. Oddly, even though it rang, there's no sound on the other end…it's still dead. Then your flashlight dies. You beat on it, but that doesn't work. At this point you really start to wonder….

You're startled by a knock at the door! You move quickly in the blackness towards it to see who might be there but you bump into a table by the end of the couch and knock it over—CRASH! The surprise terrifies you so badly you have a heart attack and die right there.

Then Harry asks, "Did the table kill you?"

Is it the table's fault you got killed? If it had been a sunny Tuesday afternoon and you had a couple friends over and you bumped into the table, surely you wouldn't have had a heart attack and expired. Bumping into the table isn't really the problem, right? It's the adverse conditions surrounding your untimely fictitious death that amplified everything to that point. Get stressed out and then it only takes one little otherwise insignificant trigger to cause a huge reaction. The same is true for horses. And that's just how Jubal-the-Massive, going along with brick hard muscles of tension from a haunted house of worries outside of his normal pastoral elements, spooks hard enough at a little bird to throw his amazingly agile rider's back out.

Horses, of course, don't reason things the way humans do. In a way, that helps us use ideal conditions to improve things with a horse. We're able to take a barn sour horse out of the barn and away from a buddy, for example, and put him in the extremely ideal conditions of a well groomed round pen just down the road a little ways. We have him in a relatively safe place that is small enough we can approach him with a conversation to seek a change and get him feeling better. The horse, however, runs circles, bucks, pushes the panels with his chest, and comes unglued. Horses possess the same life or death gravity with circumstances wherever they are, which means we can put horses in ideal settings, bring up these troubles, and address them right there as safely as possible.

Jan Bellin, from Idaho, and her mare, Nugget, take on the challenge of the crushed plastic bottle pit, one of many obstacles in the playground at Kootenai Creek Equestrian Center where Harry is hosted in Montana each summer. *(Tom Moates)*

Of course, this is why round corrals, arenas, and horse playgrounds (a.k.a. horse obstacle courses) are so helpful. We humans can use those big brains of ours to work our horses in a more controlled setting to see how things can go when we start to turn the heat up and ask more from them. We can simulate all kinds of situations that mimic things out in the world before we're really faced with truly adverse conditions to see about getting and sustaining some with-you-ness before we really head out there.

Pointing out the ideal versus adverse conditions scenario, I think, is a way Harry attempts to get people to see and strongly consider the true condition of their relationship with their horses. One undercurrent of talking about it is that some folks are climbing onto horses that are so troubled it isn't safe for them to ride off anywhere. If Harry can get people to think in these terms then perhaps they will realize that their horses experience serious bouts of not-with-you-ness when asked even small things in textbook situations. Then maybe they will see that a great deal can be done to improve the situation with a horse in a safer setting before going out onto the trail.

I don't think Harry is telling people they absolutely need to stay in the round pen until their horses are at some super highly refined level, either. However, the fact that he brings this topic up during clinics underscores the many times where people would do well to get some things going better with a horse at home before even considering heading out somewhere.

I suppose I need to confuse things further in the interest of greater overall accuracy and mention that sometimes Harry actually makes the opposite point. He says on occasion that it can be helpful to go forth and give a horse a real or "real" (as in pretend "real") job.

The point Harry is making when he says, "get out and do a job with your horse," I think, is that it can change how the *rider* presents things. That's the difference, not that the horse needs to be here or there or anywhere in particular to find interest and immediacy in what he's doing with a person. Riding to the mailbox or checking a fence are great ways for the rider to have a destination in mind involving a purpose to solidify how he presents where he wants to line out and lead the horse. If the horse senses urgency and focus in the rider, that difference often gains his thought and willingness to go somewhere specific with an impetus.

This idea makes me think about how horses interact in the herd. Perhaps you've been around a group of horses grazing contentedly when one picked up his head and pointed his ears in some direction. Instantly, everybody else does the same with complete focus. Better yet, consider what happens if a horse in such a herd suddenly takes a notion to split the scene. There's about a 100% chance that every other horse instantly is heading out of there, too! They're on the go with gusto even if they haven't seen what the migration is about yet, and this scenario doesn't have to be fear based. In fact, if they are drawing towards something of interest then they clearly are not fleeing from anything. There is a feel of urgency and direction passed between the horses in there which is the kind of thing a rider can share with a horse.

Even if it ends up that there was nothing to fuss about and the lead horse had a hallucination and got over it, it doesn't matter—that ripple in the herd dynamic made what happened as real to those horses in that moment as if there had been something to see. They

Ashley Durbin works on getting with-you-ness with Carol's horse, Stoney, in the ideal conditions of a round pen during the 2012 Bible/horsemanship clinic in Virginia. *(Pam Talley Stoneburner)*

would put the same effort into lining out and going somewhere in either scenario because the horse is just plain wired to be in the moment. We should try to capture that mindset and be the one with a mission in mind, remember that role, and then bring this dynamic into the ideal setting to get improvements going there with the horse.

So to summarize some of this, if a person is having poor results attempting to ride a line inside the controlled environment of an arena, going outside and hitting the trail might be a disaster with all those additional "thought magnets" in the real world.

("Thought magnet" is my term for a serious horse distraction—these are introduced and extensively explored in a chapter in *Between the Reins*.) However, having a "job" can help create focus and interest that the horse picks up on. Working on this inside the ideal settings of an arena or round pen instead of outside in the world obviously reduces the chances of a big fat wreck. I've seen Harry get it done tons of times. However, it requires some imagination on the part of the human, not the horse.

One of the great gifts I'm enjoying from being a longtime student of Harry's is that I'm beginning to understand how obvious trouble with my horses really manifests in smaller ways before the bigger things become evident. Catching those smaller trouble spots sooner allows me to get in there and work my horse through them. Get that little stuff cleared out and the big things can melt away and we never have to encounter big trouble.

If a horse has a little (or big) problem, and can't stay with you when being haltered and led out of the paddock to get saddled in the first place (i.e. my moment before heading out with Jubal to round up those cows next door), good luck on getting him with you to go ride anywhere. So, just thinking about juxtaposing what a particular horse looks like in the ideal setting versus the adverse setting might get a person thinking about these things.

Since my earliest attempts to ride I've found it hard to reconcile the balance between working horses in ideal versus adverse conditions, although I didn't think of it in exactly those terms. My desire to go out and get things done with my horses often resulted in less than desirable results. Clearly, that is a huge theme that weaves all through my series of horsemanship memoirs. The books reveal many of the difficulties I've encountered when attempting to climb aboard and push into ACT while still ill prepared. I suppose finding a balance between these two scenarios really is a pivotal focus of my ongoing horsemanship journey.

Chapter 3

(Dianne Madden)

Mister Dinky the Mule
(The Dinky Chronicles, Part One)

Honestly, Mister Dinky the Mule's entrenched troubles proved pretty profound. Our introduction consisted of me leaning against a board fence watching him tear around a little paddock in a panic, lead rope trailing along behind him.

I'd seen that scene before with horses, of course. Dinky, however, to get free from a handler, had a particular and very effective maneuver down to a fine art and it was habitual. I was told how a number of men at various times—some were brawny with plenty of horse experience—thought they'd be able to hold onto Dinky by his lead rope. Inevitably he'd pull away, get free, and go ripping around almost impossible to catch. None of these cowboys were able to hold him just by the lead rope. One fellow even sustained fairly severe rope burns across both hands from continuing to grasp the rope as it sizzled through his grip, simply not believing that the little mule was going to get away from him, which obviously he did.

When I heard these stories I had a suspicion that Dinky must be spinning a wickedly quick 180 degree turn and then be pulling straight away from the person attempting to hold the rope. Even a huge horse wanting to get away often can be deterred by a person if caught while turning to leave and while still somewhat sideways to the handler. The person takes advantage of the horse being a little off balance. Also, a rope on the halter of a somewhat longer animal provides a person a little more leverage between the front and hind end where the propulsion device is located. But once an equine has his butt facing you and wants to get away, good luck holding onto that lead rope! Even a modestly sized equine like Dinky possesses the power to pull a cart load of people straight ahead. It is unlikely a giant would be able to hold him back once he was in that position, not to mention Dinky adds to the moment absolute panic and complete commitment to tearing away.

That maneuver proved to be just what he was up to and it was only one symptom of many the mule possessed, all pointing to the much larger underlying problem that he severely distrusted humans, and for good reason. But I'm getting ahead of myself, so let me back up and properly introduce Mister Dinky the Mule before getting deeper into the details of our interactions....

It was mid-morning on July 12, 2012. At this point in my horsemanship journey, like I mentioned in the Introduction, I had been working with a few folks and their horses around here. About three weeks prior to meeting Dinky, I'd started working horses officially for hire. Dianne and Pat Madden had contacted me via e-mail the previous day about their troubled little mule.

Dinky was a dun, thus sporting a dorsal stripe and black stockings. Those leggings, however, tapered into awesome Zebra stripes midway up each of his four legs before transitioning to the more chestnutty solid coat which covered most of him. He displayed the prominent shoulder stripes from his donkey ancestors with a black tail and mane. The mane was short and bristly, standing at attention the whole length of the neck, increasing the Zebra look. Dinky sure was a handsome creature, I'll give him that.

Even before seeing Dinky for myself, I wasn't sure about taking him on as a project. The Maddens lived over in the next county, quite a ways beyond the outer geographical limit where I had planned to travel to work horses. Plus, Dinky's situation seemed to add up to more trouble in one animal than I had worked with before. Then I added to that list of quandaries that he was a mule. Quite simply, I wondered if my experience, acquired as it was mainly with horses, would provide me the kind of knowledge and horsemanship abilities necessary to aid an equine of a somewhat different biology and mindset.

The Maddens' sincere plea to find some help for Dinky quickly swayed me to go see if I could do anything for them and their mule. I really wanted to help Dinky and see what might be done to defuse their obvious concern for his future. Also, I wondered about my own abilities and wanted to know whether or not I could help such a troubled mule get to a better place. The worst that could happen, I figured (aside from getting kicked, bitten, dragged around, or run over), was that I'd take one look at Dinky, apologize that I couldn't help, and enjoy the lovely mountain scenery on the drive back home.

Dianne and Pat in their initial e-mail to me explained that they were a retired couple and had acquired Dinky to be a companion for their Tennessee Walking Horse. They were told beforehand that the mule had a "catching problem." I later learned that Dinky's former owner had trailered him from North Carolina to the Maddens' place in southwestern Virginia and dropped him off. Their e-mail said, "He had a permanent halter and chain on him that took two weeks to just get off him." When I asked what that meant exactly, Dianne explained she was referring to a combination of the difficulty catching him to try to get it off, getting him quiet enough long enough to get it unbuckled, and then removing it from where it had been in place on his hide and in his mane for so long.

The really good news in all this was that by the time I showed up, Dinky had lived with Dianne and Pat for two years. In those 24 months Dianne had worked extensively, and with some success, to try and get Dinky feeling better about things. She says she mainly used ideas from some Monty Roberts materials she came across to try and get Dinky more approachable and settled around people. After many

Mister Dinky the Mule and Tom in August, 2012. *(Dianne Madden)*

months of devoted work, she was the one person who could walk up to Dinky (at least, some of the time) and put a halter on him. She also had managed to get Dinky to where she could pick up his front feet quite well. Clearly, from what I witnessed, Dianne deserved a medal for sticking with it. Getting that much going was a huge improvement for this little guy. She also was able to lead him around as long as he was okay with going where she led. The instant he detected anything askew on his personal radar, however, he did that little spin ditty mentioned above and bolted.

During our introduction I watched Dianne simply let the rope drop several times when Dinky hit that flash point. Then she'd patiently follow him around until he finally stopped, faced her, and let her approach. She'd gather up the rope and start leading him again.

Clearly Dianne long ago realized that trying to hold onto Dinky in those moments was futile. I didn't blame her for that, either. Progress, slow though it might have been, clearly was being made towards getting the mule feeling better about being handled by a human. And she definitely didn't need to get hurt trying to do the impossible task of holding onto Dinky when he decided to leave.

Dianne, however, was perplexed to be participating in this established getaway routine. She knew it wasn't right for Dinky to decide to leave whenever he felt like it—but what could she do? As I stood there watching Dinky running here and there with that rope trailing along, I asked a few questions and the Maddens filled in some blanks for me. The mule's running off actually was secondary to their primary concern for Dinky.

The main thrust of contacting me was the extreme trouble they experienced trying to get Dinky trimmed. That was the reason all those cowboys got the chance to experience the mule's super pulling away powers in the first place. To put it into proper perspective, after being acquainted with Dinky for awhile, I began referring to his hind feet as being, "homicidally untrimmable."

This was no little problem. Clearly, Dinky had been through some extreme circumstances regarding those hind legs and feet. Dinky, however, needed to be trimmed for his health. The Maddens had tried everything they knew to do to get the mule's feet properly tended to with reasonably little stress to him and the human attempting it. This had been an ongoing effort for most of the two years he lived at their farm.

The Maddens explained that at first both their farrier and vet tried to trim Dinky. Both experienced such serious trouble with him they refused to try beyond their initial attempts. After some extensive searching, they found a local "mule guy" who was able to "handle" Dinky "somewhat." He went about trying to rope and tie the little mule so he would lie down and surrender to him. The fellow finally tied him up and laid him down but the mule relentlessly struggled against the ropes. Dinky eventually hurt himself to the point that upon getting loose—still with one hind foot untrimmed—it was evident he had injured himself. Dinky dragged a hind leg for several days and it was almost a month before his lameness cleared up. It was at this stage, simply heartbroken for Dinky and seemingly out of options, Dianne and Pat happened to hear about me and got in touch.

The paddock where I was watching Dinky and Dianne was triangular in shape. One side of the triangle was made up partly by a barn. It had a centered Dutch door which opened into an aisle way with a couple of stalls on either side. The rest of the fence, from corners near either end of the barn, ran about 200 feet tapering together until they met at the final point of the triangle (which actually wasn't a sharp point but rather a short section of fence, making this not really a triangle but a four sided triangle, a rare geometrical anomaly which only exists in my mind but hopefully you get the idea).

I spent at least 10 minutes talking with Pat and Dianne and watching Dianne interact with Dinky in the paddock. It was clear the most important thing to them was to get their mule to a point where he could have his feet trimmed. They loved Dinky and he was a fine companion for their Walking Horse, Rowdy. It was essential to them to be able to provide proper care for him, so trimming those hind feet was top priority. After taking this all in, I honestly wasn't sure where to start. I could see quite a little work needed to be done with Dinky before even thinking about getting to work on those back feet, so I figured the best thing to do was just pick somewhere to get going and keep it simple.

The start I chose was to have Dianne catch Dinky again and then see if she could hand the rope off to me. This worked remarkably well. Diane made the hand off and backed away. I was able to stand directly in front of him and pet his face. I asked for a few steps forward and he hung in there with me. I asked for a reverse step with some feel on the line and he had no idea what that was about, so I stuck in there, got a little bigger, and managed to get a rock back and tiny step—so I released for that and petted his face.

I approached him like a windmill (waving my arms over my head while shortening the lead rope until rubbing his face and head—a little deal I picked up from Harry shared in chapter 5 of *Between the Reins*). He braced his head up and kind of froze there with his eyes massively bugged out. I got to rubbing on his face, and then with the lead line asked him to look off to the left. He was really stuck, wide eyes and all, like a statue. I added some light tapping on the opposite side of his nose until his thought finally broke loose and he looked in the direction I was asking. This caused him to blink, bring his head down, notice his surroundings off to the left, and go back to breathing. Clearly Dinky experienced super quick mental withdrawals when he felt a little pressure or confusion. Already I was thinking that might be a precursor to his bolting episodes. I just kept playing with things there and tried to observe what his mind was up to.

All through this, Dinky was hard as a rock. He was incredibly tense, like he just knew he was in for another round of terrifying trouble and was just awaiting the battle to begin. Next, I moved a couple steps along the left side of his face. It was a slight, subtle move where I just was trying to get into a position where I could reach and rub the upper part of his neck, not even as far back as his withers. Just that tiny move off center was too much for Dinky. My step to his left was all it took, and I experienced his blisteringly quick 180 degree departure first hand. For the record, I put an effort into blocking the departure by putting a hold on the rope, but obviously it was not going to stop him—no surprise there. He was loose and went to the far end of the triangle.

I walked after him and moved him around the paddock at liberty for a few minutes. The space was so large I had to really hoof it to be anywhere close to Dinky. I treated the situation like we were in a round corral—putting a little pressure on him when he was most mentally gone to get him searching and seeking to have him consider thinking my way. The paddock was just too big for me to be very effective in establishing some kind of conversation with a mule so convinced of how terrible things are about to get. I played with this for a few minutes while talking to the Maddens about what I was doing and what I saw in Dinky.

A 40 foot lariat with a ring instead of a honda was in my car. I thought about it and then had an idea. My thought was to get the lariat onto Dinky's neck and see if I could use that 40 feet of rope to improve my chances of establishing better communication. I knew the scenario with him would start out the same, so as I got into

At first, Dinky was very worried and frequently braced his neck with muscles hard as a rock. *(Dianne Madden)*

trouble spots with Dinky (which were caused by doing pretty much anything with him at this point) he'd be headed for the horizon. Hopefully the extra length of rope would provide me a much greater opportunity to get him turned after he squirted away. Or it might at least help to get things going again more quickly after a panic attack subsided, since I might still have my hands on the rope.

I had Dianne come back in and with her magic touch get a hold of Dinky. Then I was able to approach those two with the lariat, get a loop over his head, and Dianne unclipped the lead rope. She slipped away and I was there facing Dinky with the rope now around his neck. I was able to approach him head-on but again, as soon as I went slightly to the side, he bolted. I reeled out coils and trailed along behind him.

Even with 40 feet of rope I quickly had all my coils out and was hanging onto the end of the rope and running for all I was worth looking like a kid holding the end of a kite string getting dragged along. I barely held on to where Dinky finally was stopped by the far point of the triangle fence.

I regained my balance and put a little feel on the line. It was interesting to watch the mule's reaction. He readily turned, stood for a second realizing we were still connected by the rope (albeit by a long distance), and then walked quietly towards me as I reeled him in. The panic seemed to be instantly over and it was as if he said, "Oh, you've still got the lead rope, well okay then, here I come."

My hope was that, since it was very unlikely my timing and skill would allow me to stay ahead of his 180 departure, the next best thing was to let him do it but have it not work out so well. He'd still be blowing away from me whenever he felt the need but not be completely free from me like he had been managing with the shorter rope. Not only would this be way easier on me not chasing a loose mule all over creation, but perhaps he might just let go of the desire to run off in the first place learning it was a futile exercise. That, along with consistently offering a calm, reassuring, and sweet spot for him every time I reeled him in again, I hoped might begin to build some trust in him.

It was a great theory, and I only had a little time to play with it before I had to wrap things up that first day. Several times while Dinky was close to me I was very keen to work on gaining his thought and direct it for small things—like asking him to look in a direction or step a front foot slightly to the side rather than always just straight ahead. I began to see how hard it was for him to be present with me but how it brought some clarity and even slight relaxation at moments when achieved. I'd never worked with any equine quite like Dinky before, and it was exhilarating to have managed even a few moments of positive change that first day.

Many little things happened in that short session but what excited me the most was beginning to establish some consistent handling with Dinky. Already I'd begun to work on eliminating any confusion between us. In everything I asked of Dinky, I tried my very best to do as Harry says, "mean what you say and say what you mean." When I presented some feel to him I wanted him to be able to bank on the fact that there was an answer in it, a clarity, and he need not be fearful but simply search and find it. That no matter what everything will be okay, and it'll always be the very best when with me.

As this began to work between us a bit even in that short time, I began to get a sense he was thinking about another thing I've heard Harry say, "It can't be this simple!" His experiences convinced him absolutely that people are confusing and then they get angry. Next, he finds himself confined and in serious trouble and never understands why. How can this new person calmly and without irritation ask something of him and he be able to find it, do it, and that's all there is to it? He gets a pet on the face and a big smile from the human. Nothing but the very opposite of this, I believe, had been proven to this mule his entire life.

Dinky long ago gave up trying to see what people might be asking of him, I think. Dinky's reality, I saw, was uncertainty resulting from a lifetime of mixed messages and very inconsistent handling, ending in many unpleasant reactions from humans. This, no doubt, was a huge factor in his mental shutdowns and bolting.

I thought about Dinky constantly after that first meeting and was eager to go back. The Maddens agreed to have me come out again and would have had me back the very next week, but I was flying out to catch up with Harry in Minnesota and then travel with him across the northwest to attend a couple of his clinics. That trip gave me time to visit with Harry about Dinky, which helped me reflect on what I'd seen and what to try next. And I already was scheduled to go out and work with the mule again upon my return.

But I'll come back to Dinky a little later.... Next, speaking of that trip traveling with Harry out west, I had the opportunity to take in his Montana clinic and there's some things from it I'm eager to share.

Chapter 4

(Jan Bellin)

Free Searching with Sunshine in Montana

Crack! The sharp noise hit me like a dart in the forehead.

I saw a tall cowboy wielding a stock whip standing centered in the confines of a round corral. A Morgan mare ran hard out on the rail—head up, looking out, and thinking about being elsewhere.

I watched every movement as things unfolded. The horse whizzed around and the fellow unfurled the whip out in front of him again.

Crack!

Okay, don't worry, it was Harry in there with the whip. He was working with Linda Davenport's horse, Sunshine, during a clinic hosted by Malika Coston in Stevensville, Montana in August 2012. The round pen was constructed of pine poles and was situated on a flat that rose slightly for maybe half a mile where it met the backdrop of a rolling ridge in the Bitterroot Mountains.

The whole scene simply smacked of the old west. Harry, for once chap-less, wore his well worn high-topper boots, a red shirt, and straw cowboy hat. Were it not for the microphone and small headset draped around his collar, the image it created could have been from any time in the past century and a half.

Sunshine shone a coat color in the sunlight that I'd never seen before. Later Linda explained to me that she is a "sooty palomino." It's a color caused by a special gene in some of the palomino strains that causes counter shading on top of the palomino color and silvering of the mane and tail.

Linda brought a strong curiosity about setting up searches in horses to the clinic with her. She asked quite a few questions about the idea of "free searches" discussed in *Further Along the Trail* (the book preceding this one in the series) which was released earlier that year. A "free search" really is just setting up a search in a horse—that is, providing any kind of "ask" which gets the horse looking for what a person wants.

The "free" part gets added in there sometimes simply to stress that a horse is going to be given a ton of time and room to roam at liberty, like in a round pen or arena, to go searching for what a person wants. Also, it speaks to the point that the person will attempt to avoid intentionally directing the horse. The person tries only to do the one thing (like whacking a whip on the ground or flipping a flag) which is meant to break loose a horse's thought from elsewhere and keep them searching for the ultimate goal that the person has in mind (like stepping on a tarp or entering an open trailer). Linda asked if Harry would do one during the clinic that week, and Harry agreed to use one of her sessions at the end of a day to set up one of these searches with Sunshine.

Linda had traveled to the clinic with her friend, Jan Bellin, from back home in Idaho. Jan also was riding in the clinic, and Sunshine clearly showed an affinity for being near Jan's horse. The round pen was way across the field from where the horses were being kept in outside stalls. Linda put Sunshine in the round pen with Harry and it was easy to see the mare's thoughts were clear back with her buddy. Harry explained he was going to set the search up for Sunshine to come to him in the middle of the pen and be feeling soft and relaxed about it.

I have to say, just the thought of someone cracking a whip in close confines with a horse that's already troubled and running around is naturally a little unnerving if you care about these creatures. One might think that such a loud and imposing tool as a stock whip only would increase a worried horse's inner turmoil no matter what. If I didn't know Harry, that's exactly what I'd expect! Harry, however, used this scenario as a chance to bring a horse through a search to feeling better about some things. His choice of gear for the job, I think (I'm not sure if it was intentional or not), really provoked us onlookers to consider that what tool is used to get horse searching for an answer is far less critical than the timing and feel of how something is presented to the horse.

Even with the big *crack!*, the mare didn't really pay much attention to Harry at first. She was romping around and concentrating on her friend across the field. It provided a perfectly observable example of a horse's thought being elsewhere—you could all but see Sunshine's brain jump out of her head and bounce over the corral fence and roll up the hill to be with Jan's horse. Harry took stock of the situation, and as the mare ran circles around the pen and

Harry cracks the stock whip as Sunshine passes—the Bitterroot Mountains loom large in the background. *(Tom Moates)*

passed a certain point he'd chosen, he took that whip and again, *crack*!

Sunshine took more notice this time but kept going. As she tore past that same point again, *crack*!

Sunshine's brain came back into the corral this time. She focused on Harry, turned toward the clinician, and halted at a distance right behind him. Harry had been just standing there looking in one direction, doing nothing more than letting the whip fly once in awhile. For the first time, she let go of thinking about how to get her body to her buddy for a moment and started checking out this cowboy to see what he was up to. Her attention on Harry wasn't very strong at this point. I wondered how much of approaching Harry from behind him had to do with being behind the human and how much of that position had to do with still keeping an eye on her buddy who was now in the direction that Sunshine faced. She couldn't remain standing there for long, and soon she was out running on the rail again.

In my clinic notes from that session I recorded my impressions saying, "There seems to be a conformity to Sunshine's initial stops but when Harry asked her to be there—to have her thought be with him—she had to leave town. Conformity, not willing and ready. Shallow, just giving him a piece, not her full self."

Harry spoke to us spectators as things unfolded in the round corral. One of the things he pointed out was how hard it is for many horses to let go of a strong thought like that which Sunshine had for her buddy. This kind of trouble in a horse isn't motivated by a simple, "Oh, I'd sure rather be up there in my pen." This kind of intensive focus out of the pen is related to the very core nature of a horse preserving its life.

I think he meant that what Sunshine was experiencing was more along the lines of what a person might feel if they'd been nabbed right off the sidewalk when walking with a friend, thrown into a vehicle, and whisked away kidnapped. If you were in that car with those kidnappers, how would you feel as you watched out the window as your friend disappeared from view? I think that's the kind of fright a horse feels in this situation.

Harry didn't use that example, that's just how I think about it sometimes, but he expressed plainly that a horse like Sunshine can't let that go because it's more of a life-and-death situation to her. We can miss that. Humans may think, "Silly horse, cut that out. We're only just going over here to this corral." But the horse doesn't know this. They're in the moment and at that moment separation from a buddy and going across the field is extremely worrisome. Harry adds

Sunshine still runs on the rail as Harry continues a conversation with her. *(Tom Moates)*

in there that to a horse like Sunshine, feeling and acting this way has worked to preserve her life so far—in her mind, it has been proven beyond any doubt that it is what she needs to do to keep surviving according to her experiences to date. And if a person can break that thought pattern and show the horse she can feel better by thinking right there with him, then he has helped support her to a much better place she didn't realize existed.

Next in my clinic journal about this session I wrote, "It's not about whether the horse can stop running around and come in and approach you, but rather can the horse feel good about stopping and coming in to be with you?"

"As I recall," Linda e-mailed me about it later, "she then sort of relaxed a little, and he let her stay there and get comfortable for a minute or two (while she was behind him still at a distance), and then he cracked the whip in front of him. She left again, took a trip or two around, and, this time, stopped right in front of him. Harry just stood there, sort of looking at the ground; she stood there with her head and neck up, studying him. Then she boldly walked up to Harry, and as he stuck out his hand to pet her nose, she poked her nose out at him, so he let her run into the tip of his finger. Off for another trip.

"Then, she came back and stood in front of him, near the railing, and got comfortable. He let her stand there for a few minutes, and then he just raised the whip a little, and she dropped her head and slowly, one step at a time, came right on in to Harry. And this time, she did not poke her nose at him. At this point I had tears in my eyes, I must say. It was beautiful. She'd found the place of peace."

The search went on for more than an hour, so the above makes it seem quicker than it really was. Sunshine put in quite an effort searching for what Harry was asking and it was no small thing for her to let go of her other thought to try to find what he was offering. She first had to realize another option to her regular mode existed. Then she had to dip her hoof into that puddle to test the waters.

Increasingly, she became convinced that she could let go of her thought and try other things. Since Harry was not blocking her from trying anything in that round corral, she totally owned the decision to look him up when she considered it herself. There was no resentment in that; how could there be? Harry hadn't cornered her into trying only one thing. Instead, he just asked her to break loose her mental grip on other things like trying to get her body outside the pen. He knew from experience that with the timing of his asks (whip cracks) she eventually would try what he had in mind, so he just let her work at that awhile to see what she did.

One aspect of Sunshine's search that really sticks with me is included in the observation Linda made above. It is the fact that Harry let the mare bump into his finger, which I'm sure he knew full well could (and did) cause her to leave him again. And he allowed this to happen even though it was her first time coming in close to him. He made the choice not to allow her to approach him by pushing her nose into his space although the search was set up to ask her (physically) to come up to him. Harry wasn't just accepting the physical but also was insisting on her coming up to him with very good feelings.

"What's really interesting to me in the picture of her standing right behind Harry," says Linda Davenport, "is not only her facial expression and obvious thoughts on Harry, but see her tail? It's crooked. It seems to me she's at a very high level of, 'What the heck is going on here? He's not chasing me—he wants something. I'm not sure what, but I'm sure enough ready to leave in a split second.' Definitely searching." *(Jan Bellin)*

Reflecting on that moment, I wondered what I would have done there. Honestly, I was thinking I'd be so delighted she finally was coming to me that I'd have taken it and rubbed her face in praise. But the crux of the search was for Harry to get her feeling the best he could. Even though that bump sent her out again and away from the "physical goal" of getting her there with Harry, I could see that in the bigger picture not letting her come in and push on the person actually got her feeling better sooner.

In other words, Harry didn't settle for her coming all the way up to him even one time while being pushy, feeling pinched up, or having her thoughts anywhere else. Am I willing to settle for less? I hope not, but when I see Harry work a horse I often see places like this where I know I'd either miss those little expressions of not-with-you-ness, or I'd settle for less than I should thinking I'd better take what I can at first. Is coming in, even pushy or snarky, "the slightest try" which should be rewarded?

The result of Sunshine's free search is my answer to this question. If I clear up something like that little pushy nose right up front, the next time she comes around it may very well be gone, and gone for good. One thing is for sure, if I don't ever allow it then it won't ever happen in the first place. On the other hand, if I take it, I still may be able to go on and work through that as things improve, but pushiness is pushiness. If she got by with it from the very first

By the end of the search, Sunshine let go of her other thoughts and was soft and contented to come in and stand by Harry. *(Tom Moates)*

time she came into me, then that may stick with her and she may try that for a long time.

Perhaps Linda sums it up best. She said to me about Sunshine's search, "It's discovering how much a horse will offer if you give them an opportunity. They will, given the opportunity, search for the answer to what you're offering without the necessity of you driving them to the answer. It's quite amazing to see the obvious peace that comes over them. I have a much, much greater appreciation of what's been there before me all those years, but I didn't quite see that!"

Chapter 5

(Carol Moates)

Trailer Loading Mirage

It happened twice. Two fillies in two years trained to trailer load in two minutes! The first one, a two year old, hopped in that metal box literally in two minutes without a hint of trouble. The second one, a yearling, didn't step up all the way in until day two, but the whole process unfolded with such a lack of trouble or ill feelings it might as well have been two minutes.

The first one was Minnie, Carol's bay crop out Paint filly who was sold to a fellow here in the area. She was so easy to load from the start that she's a terrible example to share, so I'll just skip that one for now.

The next year, another bay filly of Carol's, Mirage, needed to learn to load. After this second straight forward trailer loading experience, the term "non-event" really stuck in my head. A non-event is when a horse is with you, follows the feel you present, you both get where you'd like to go together, and there simply are no ripples on the water of undertaking a task. Something gets done in such a sweetly flowing way that on the horsemanship scale of 1 (sweetest possible) to 10 (human takes a trip to hospital) it registers about a 1.457.

Considering these two experiences got me thinking about how we humans are responsible for the bulk of the trouble that our horses end up with in the horse/human relationship. Likewise, it made me contemplate how one can set things up to minimize or eliminate the horse feeling bad about many experiences with people. There's hardly a better example to show where people build bad experiences into a relationship with horses than loading them into trailers.

When mulling over this idea, for some reason, I immediately imagined what uninitiated onlookers (to the horse world) must think of a non-event. Perhaps to them, for example, having a colt come up with calm attention and offer to place his head in a halter for a person to snug up and tie in place may just seem to be how these things work. It may not register to those unfamiliar with horsemanship that it is noteworthy that nothing extra and undesired happened right then.

If a person starts with a typical youngster and no trouble ever gets exchanged in the first place, then sure...that should be a matter-of-fact progression that lacks any problems. Why wouldn't it be? But on the other hand, if you don't know how not-with-you a horse that's had bad experiences with a person can be—like with poor Dinky where people can't get close to him in the pasture, let alone get him haltered—then you just don't know. Average folks can't be expected to recognize and admire a non-event for the simple sublime horse/human interaction it represents. After all, that's the thing about a non-event, it's largely about what *didn't* just happen!

However, to those who have suffered through some actual events when handling horses and worked for years to get to the point where they can make interacting with a horse look easy and uneventful, observing or participating in a non-event packs a good bit of appreciation.

"Did you see that!" I imagine the horse-obsessed individual might blurt out to an uninitiated onlooker friend.

"What?"

"How she haltered that colt."

"Well, yeah...I saw she just put the halter on him. So? Did something happen?"

"No...nothing happened! That colt approached softly, lined up, lowered his head, and slipped his nose into it...amazing! She's done a great job with him."

"Yeah, okay...so what's the horse supposed to do (you idiot)?

How about Mexican for lunch?"

The recent trailer loading sessions with Mirage provide a pretty good example of what I think goes into setting up a non-event. Non-events don't just happen on their own, after all. They require effort, forethought, preparation, several years of serious study, and surviving many actual events. And this was my favorite kind of non-event, one that unfolded with a young horse as I worked through the introductory experiences of handling her in a new situation.

Honestly, for the record, I find working with foals and previously unhandled horses more stressful than working with horses that pack around some human interaction baggage. It is kind of nerve wracking to be responsible for each new handling experience that the young horse has. Any problems that get built in there, I only have myself to blame for them. It is a huge responsibility. Still, I love working with them, especially once things get in motion and start to shape up. Then my mind focuses on keeping their thoughts with me, working with bringing them and their minds along to whatever we're doing, and the voice of worry melts away in the moment.

By contrast, give me a horse that's been all messed up at the hands of humans and I don't think twice about getting in there to see what trouble lurks and what I might do to help the horse get to feeling better about things. Interacting with people is a bad experience for that kind of a horse, but it's not my fault.

Mirage was not quite a year and a half old at the time of this example. She is a well built and pretty sensible filly. There never was a wreck along the way as we started haltering and leading her. Basic handling was going okay by the time of this particular non-event.

The filly had been weaned for about a year and was living

with Stoney, Carol's spotty leopard Appaloosa gelding. It was summer and the pair were getting rotated around to graze various smallish paddocks on our place. The opportunity opened up for some excellent and more expansive pasture at a friend's farm about seven miles away. The Big-Uns had been turned out over there for several weeks and hadn't made a dent in the forage yet. We decided these other two ought to go as well and stay through the fall since the grass was so abundant. This would mean a trailer ride, and Mirage had yet to be introduce to a metal box on wheels. So, it was trailer loading teaching time.

Our friend, Derrick, has a 20 foot stock trailer and offered to let me use it for starting Mirage to load. It was the same one I used with Minnie the previous year and it is a perfect trailer for the task. It's very spacious, reducing the claustrophobia some small, enclosed trailers seem to promote. The whole back end is a door that swings open, or you can slide open a smaller door half that size built within it allowing for a variety of loading scenarios. Along the sides there is a single open slat at about the horse's eye level. The rest of the sides are solid providing a nice balance between open and enclosed space. It sports a rubber mat floor which seems to lessen spooky noises by muffling the metallic racket inside the trailer and provides nice footing. There's even a middle partition that swings closed to split the long trailer in two for challenging a horse in different ways while training.

It was June and the weather had turned very hot. Mirage and Stoney were in a paddock near the entrance to our farm. Just outside their gate was a level, graveled area where Derrick parked the trailer. Large trees shaded it in the morning and late afternoon. With the temperature and humidity in a race to see who could reach 95 first each day, I figured on working with the filly each morning during the cooler, shady spells.

To start, I unlatched the back gate of the trailer and swung it wide open. Stoney is a very easy loader, so I got Carol to halter him and walk him into the trailer and hang out up in the front of it. I figured it couldn't hurt for Mirage to see her uncle Stoney up in there calmly standing and hoped he might increase her draw and curiosity to think into the trailer.

Tom offers feel on the lead rope for Mirage to think up in the trailer.
(Carol Moates)

I'd conducted plenty of trailer loadings and seen Harry get problem loaders going better into trailers at clinics many times. From the start, I set it up so the filly would search to get into the trailer and avoided boxing her in without other choices. Or, to say it differently, I wanted it to be her idea to check out the trailer, follow a feel and step up in there rather than forcing the issue and having her flee into the trailer away from me.

With Carol and Stoney situated up in the front of the gooseneck to act as beings of interest, I led Mirage to the open end of the trailer. At first I stood on the ground by the left corner of the trailer. The filly was pretty good about following the feel of the lead rope if I'd ask her to step forward, back, to the side, or go out to circle me. Using what we had going for us, I asked her to step up to the back bumper and look inside with her feet remaining on the ground. She was curious enough that it didn't take much and I instantly released and rubbed on her when she did it.

We hung out there as long as she kept thinking into the trailer. She sniffed the floor and bit the rubber matting a little to satisfy her curiosity, which I didn't interrupt at that early stage. Before long her mind drifted away from the trailer. I blocked those wayward thoughts by putting a little feel on the rope.

Occasionally, I resorted to slapping my chap with the end of the lead rope to provide a little extra emphasis to get her mind loose from other thoughts and to come back to the task at hand. If she was thinking about the inside of that trailer, however, I let her relax there. I was careful not to be in a hurry, drive her forward, or to insist that she get in.

Mirage eventually stepped one foot onto the trailer floor and pawed at the rubber matting curiously. I presented a feel for her to think in there deeper. She stepped both front feet up onto the trailer floor and stood there before stepping back down. That scenario repeated a few times. She wasn't readily going in any further. We worked there for about 30 minutes. I was in no hurry and decided to be content with that progress for the day. Carol and I turned both horses out to pasture again and went home for lunch.

Sure, getting the filly into the trailer could have been accomplished more quickly—likely even in less time than I spent playing around there that first morning. It could have been handled poorly but more quickly if the goal was just to get her in there rather than to build the positive experience of her loading willingly. Two guys locking arms around her behind, throwing the young horse in, and slamming the door would be quick, the negative consequences of which you don't have to look very far in the horse world to see, ranging from residual resentment when loading to ongoing outright trailer terror and a lifetime of recurring refusal to load.

It also might have been handled well but more quickly if, for instance, Harry had done it and chose to work it that way. Which, from the vantage point where I now stand in my horsemanship journey, I'd say would amount to the horse being offered many options to consider, figuring out they won't work out as good as this other thing the human says will work best, and then being perfectly content in a short time to happily go where Harry suggests.

I'm improving with this kind of presentation, but I still work best with lots of time to let the horse search. I'm forever fascinated with how their minds go here and there, how I can guide them to let other things go, and ultimately how I can help them trim down their options to what I set out for them to achieve. And most importantly, to get all that in an increasingly relaxed way, one that hopefully they feel like was a choice they made.

But by watching Harry (Ray Hunt is another stellar example of a horseman I witnessed get a whole conversation with a horse into a very short time) I began to grasp that ultimately it's really not about the amount of time taken to get something done with a horse—it's all about the timing of how it's undertaken.

With Mirage, my goal towards trailer loading being a non-event was well underway. Plans with horses don't always work out the way you hope, of course, but for this trailer loading lesson, I had a plan. I had a good spot picked out to work in and a great trailer to work with. There were no time constraints on our situation—a point which really was more about me not getting pinched up inside feeling the need to rush things. I expected good results with Mirage, more or less, and was ready to watch closely to notice anything that ran counter to them that would indicate unanticipated trouble in the filly.

That first experience ended up all positive as far as I could tell. There were no wrecks or big fearful episodes. She was curious. I hadn't let her thoughts wander away to where she wallowed around mentally to find trouble—as Harry says, "It's amazing what a horse won't do if you don't let him." The first look into a trailer was no big deal and nothing happened to hurt, spook, or trap her. That's a fine step in the right direction, I figured—let her search it out at this slow pace as long as I keep her searching.

The next morning I repeated the scenario with Carol and Stoney in the front of the trailer and me at the back with Mirage. I started by putting some feel on the lead rope to ask her to think inside the trailer. She put a foot up on the floor quickly this time and pawed the rubber quite a bit. Before long she had both front feet up there and was checking out the inside more intently. After letting her be there a minute and rubbing on her, I backed her onto the ground, got a flag, and worked her a little with the flag in the area behind the trailer. I had her circle me both ways, back up, come forward…just keeping her thought with me and worked on sending it (and her) on a line here and there. Then I went back to the trailer and asked her to consider going inside.

She quickly and willingly stepped her front half into the trailer and spent a little while there but going no further. Then I gave a little flagging action off to her side and she stepped right up in the trailer.

I never drove her forward with the flag. That is something I've learned from Harry and repeat often because it can't be overstressed. I simply added some flagging to the situation when she had a thought of standing there half in until she let that thought go and considered going forward all the way into the trailer. And she went in softly as you please.

Now inside, I gave her some really fine loving and rubbing. She checked out her buddy, Stoney, and Carol. There was no detectable apprehension about the trailer itself once she was in there. It was as if she'd kind of worked that out already during her time standing at the back and peering inside. After a few minutes of chilling in the trailer (if you can call it that at near 90 degrees) I brought her thought around, turned her, and asked her out of the trailer head first.

She was more hesitant about stepping out of the trailer than any other part of the experience. The step down onto the ground was troubling to her at first. Ever since the first time she walked fully into the trailer, though, she has never hesitated to load. We went in and out of the trailer a few times for good measure, with her exit improving each time, and called it a day.

On the third day Mirage and I did another session, without Carol and Stoney in the trailer this time. It was no problem at all, a complete non-event! She walked right up in there the first time I asked. Then we spent some time in the trailer. I turned her around

Mirage was more uncertain about stepping back out of the trailer at first than climbing up into it. *(Carol Moates)*

in there, played with closing the center partition, and clanged around on the metal sides and roof—it all went great. I took time to unload her by backing her out as well as stepping out forward, both of which went great. Then I closed the big rear door and practiced, with no problem, loading her through the smaller sliding door that's build into it. It was FUN!

A few days later, Derrick came by with his dually and we hooked up the trailer. Mirage and Stoney loaded without a hint of hesitation, and up the road they went to the new pasture. They unloaded fine and got turned out into waist deep grass across a fence

On the third day, the filly stepped right up in the trailer when asked.
(Carol Moates)

from the Big-Uns. There they stayed until the end of September when it was time for the 2012 Bible/horsemanship clinic with Ronnie Moyer and Harry that we host here in Floyd, Virginia each year.

Ashley Durbin, one of the six clinic riders that year, recently had moved from Tennessee to Baton Rouge, Louisiana. Her truck died the week before the clinic, which scuttled her hopes of bringing her horse, so we offered Stoney for her to ride instead. I planned to ride the Bigs (both Festus and Jubal) during the clinic on different days, depending on how things went. Also, I was thinking about getting Harry to work with Mirage in one of my riding slots that week. As it turned out, I needed to trailer all four horses home for the clinic, which was being held on a farm adjacent to our place.

Mirage and Stoney had been handled very little all summer. Derrick was helping me set things up for the clinic and was riding in it, as well. He offered to haul all four horses together in his stock trailer. When we went to fetch them we parked, opened the trailer, and decided to load Mirage and Stoney first. That filly led out the gate, across a driveway, and walked right up in that trailer with me like she did it every day of her life. She stood calmly inside while Derrick loaded Stoney next. Then we closed the center partition, put Festus and Jubal in the back, and drove to the clinic. Loading Mirage that day proved to be a total non-event.

The example, I think, is a good one to consider regarding how to approach new things with a horse (trailer loading, saddling, bridling...anything) so that negative events never are given the chance to get established in the first place. And I was delighted that after some months, Mirage still felt the same about loading in the trailer as the day she had been delivered to that pasture. I don't have any

Stoney enjoying turn-out at the 2012 Virginia Bible/horsemanship clinic.
(Pam Talley Stoneburner)

reason to think she wouldn't have, but like I said earlier, if you've ever suffered through some actual events with horses, you sometimes appreciate the non-events for being just that!

Mirage, it seems, has a great beginning towards a lifetime of trailer loading non-events. Minnie, before her, went more quickly, which I think was due to the fact that more work was done with her in general ahead of trailer loading. Now when I work with an inexperienced horse to do something it's never done before, like trailer loading, I think about making it a non-event. Of course, with the Jubals and Dinkys in our lives, that isn't really possible since there is trouble inside of them already that we must bring up so that we can work with it and get them past it. But with colts and horses without much handling, we can do much to set things up so we progress positively, keeping them with us from the very start.

Chapter 6

(Dianne Madden)

Dinky Days
(The Dinky Chronicles, Part Two)

The second time I went to work with Mister Dinky the Mule was soon after returning from my two week trip out west with Harry. It was August 14th, 2012. Dianne and Pat had me come out for two hours instead of one—partly it provided me more working time for the long drive, and they realized it was going to require a lot of time to get Dinky feeling better about some things if we were going to work on picking up those hind feet. I was very glad for a serious chance to see if I could help him.

When I pulled up for my second session, I saw that Pat had run a rope across the paddock between two posts which cut the triangle in half (thus isolating the pointy end and making a smaller quadrangle space to work in at the other end by the barn). The quadrangle is where Dinky stood in halter and rope with Dianne when I arrived. The space still was much larger than a typical round pen but certainly more manageable than having that whole triangle space open.

After just one meeting, already I knew Dinky was complicated and completely convinced people (especially cowboys holding ropes) were out to harm him. It was plain to see this mule held onto his established patterns to a greater extent than any horse I'd worked with before. He withheld his "tries" (for lack of a better way of saying it) to the bitter end. It required incredible persistence to instigate any search and get even a slight try out of him. To complicate matters further, on the other hand, an ounce too much pressure with the presentation and he spun a 180 degree turn and all I saw were his tail lights in the distance.

Earlier in my horsemanship journey there's no way I could have been much help to Dinky. I simply did not possess the confidence to know that what I presented would be understood and that he'd come through and even give a try. I wouldn't have held out with my "asks" for the inordinately long time it took to get him searching and then come through with a change—even a small one.

Likewise, when he bolted, I'd have felt like I'd blown my chances to get it right and was making things worse and been completely depressed about it. Even in the first session with Dinky, I saw beyond those old worries and knew I was starting to get somewhere with him, albeit very tiny steps. Also, I'd seen enough work with troubled horses that I knew this mule already was so bothered that there was no need to be distracted with the worry that his ripping away occasionally was going to make anything worse at this point.

So I got right in there and started playing with all the things that bugged him, which was pretty much everything. I kept poking into these problem areas to prove to him there's no need to be worried about them. I'd rub his face, then let my hand slide up and touch his big mule ears. Oh, he hated that, so I did a bunch of it. Then I started to flop those ears around quite often—not mean spirited, mind you, but with the feel of a little kid who is a good friend just picking at him for fun. At first, he was truly terrified and it amounted to one more reason to tear away to the far reaches of the paddock. But as time went on he let me do more and more ear flopping without expending all the energy it took to run off just to get reeled back in again.

To tell you the truth, at first the ears were absolute powder kegs of worry with Dinky. This was similar to my experience with Jubal (The Wonder Horse) when he came to me. I noticed that both of these guys felt worry about their left ears in particular. It's impossible to know for sure, but I chalked this up to being ear twitched and figured since mainstream horse folk typically do everything from the horse's left side it is likely the left ear was the first thing they went to grab to subdue the beasts when bridling, giving dewormer, or whatever.

Before long, my good hearted, persistent antagonizing had Dinky hanging in there taking a whole bunch of ear flopping without running off. He'd try to move his handsome head as far away from my hand as possible without actually moving a foot. Then swing it back the other way and stretch to try and avoid my hand but (*flop, flop, flop*) to no avail. He mostly just was perturbed now with me, not terrified. I believe the change came because the action with his ears never escalated to anything worse with me, it just amounted to

Mister Dinky the Mule. *(Dianne Madden)*

ear flopping with no ulterior motive. Plus, I always tried to hang in there until I saw a change in him towards a better feeling before quitting flopping.

Occasionally he even managed to relax and enjoy a few moments of ear massage before he remembered he had to be worried about it. It also became a very good place for me to begin to notice the difference between Dinky being with me and present (alert to his surroundings), and him shutting down and withdrawing his thoughts inside himself. The change was so subtle with Dinky sometimes that I had to make a move or touch an ear to see if he reacted to know for sure which stage he was in.

Dinky was the hardest creature I'd ever come across to convince to make a lasting mental change. He needed to be shown over and over and over again that even the little things happening between us could be okay. Just the minutia of stepping a front foot slightly to the side (instead of straight forward) in response to the feel I presented on the rope took considerable time and effort. It seemed he only knew about taking straight forward steps, period. Any deviation from a strict march ahead when connected to a human by a lead rope was not even in his category of possibilities.

Similarly, I had trouble getting him to allow me to come even a few inches alongside his head to rub further down his neck. He acted like any variance from only the most rigid positions literally would kill him—like he was standing on a small chunk of ice floating in the water and sharks were circling ready for him to fall in at any second, so he was taking no chances!

It reminds me of an example Harry uses sometimes to get people to consider how deeply horses experience their realities and illustrate the profound nature of what we are up against when we try to help them.

"What if you went to the doctor and he told you that if your left shoulder gets bumped into you'll die?" Harry asks. "So you go get a second opinion, and that doctor says the same thing. You try for a third opinion, and that one says, 'Yep, if that shoulder gets knocked into it'll kill you!' How would that belief change your behavior as you went through life from then on? Even if it really wasn't true, you'd be deeply affected by those professional opinions. Protecting that shoulder would become an all consuming concern with everything you did, wouldn't it!"

Dinky knew without a doubt that if a person got to fooling with his hind feet it could kill him. Experience taught him that's when things get really bad, people get angry, tie him up, probably thump him…there's no telling what all he has experienced. His whole reality now sits built on this foundation of protecting his hind parts. This was not a deal where he was kind of irritable about his back end, no—this was self preservation to the core. As I began to work on touching him a little closer to the withers he tensed so much that his neck was locked upwards and was hard as a rock. Before long, he began to drip sweat all over his body as he stood there.

From the Maddens' eyewitness accounts of Dinky's previous encounters with cowboys and farriers, along with the level of trouble I had seen in the little fellow so far, I knew that if anyone went to grab a hind foot he was going to get kicked. There would be no warning shot over the bow, Dinky would straight up sink your dingy. And we weren't even close to trying to get to the hind feet yet.

Mostly at this point I was sure glad he showed no propensity to bite, although Dianne had warned me of that possibility! Again, none of these concerns were from any meanness or aggressive tendencies I detected in the mule. It was just that I knew approaching the inner turmoil he possessed, which was necessary to help him jettison the horrible baggage he carried, would certainly bring out his survival mechanisms when I accidentally went too far and tipped him over the line. To add to Dinky's turmoil, anything confusing to him created a similar kind of worry. He definitely took to fleeing instead of fighting whenever he could.

Harry spoke about a horse problem during the recent clinic I attended in Montana that related to Dinky's kind of trouble. He explained that in situations like Dinky presented, we aren't trying to change habits in the horse but rather we are working to change a *whole belief system*. The horse knows what he knows because it has been proven to him as an absolute fact. Thus to get a true change in his feelings about something we have to *prove* to him things are otherwise. Horses are experiential creatures, so to talk with them about this kind of thing we must go to these places physically to have the conversation. Harry added that it is not easy, that the horse has to gain trust in us, and we must speak to the horse using experiences that absolutely confirm the change and open a world of new possibilities.

With persistence, Dinky started to build a new understanding with me in some areas. At first, the changes were incredibly slight and Dinky wasn't offering me much to work with. I did my best to explain to Dianne and Pat what I was seeing in their mule and what I was doing as things unfolded.

I went ahead and worked Dinky at liberty for awhile in the

now smaller lot. I grabbed the 40 foot rope on my way in figuring I'd soon pick up where I left off last time, with a loop around his neck and plenty of length to let him run off when he needed to without getting totally loose. In the meantime, I used the coiled lariat to slap my chaps to get his mind moving when his thoughts got stuck or left the paddock altogether.

He began to pass closer to me at times, but I felt there was no doubt it would be a really, really long search before he ever came up to me and stopped. Fast-forwarding over many months now, we're still working on this. I've become pretty certain that most horses, even very troubled horses, would have tried coming in and being with me long ago. Dinky has offered to come in to me close enough so I could stroke his face only twice in all this time. I think it may be a mule trait that he can go so incredibly long without putting closeness to the human as an option on the table. People long ago sized mules up as just being stubborn but the truth is, if a mule gets convinced of something he doesn't forgive and forget where it seems a horse often will. So, back to Dinky Day number two. I had Dianne come in with her magic touch and catch him by the halter. I placed the loop of my lariat over his head and onto his neck and she slipped away.

Dinky could hang in there when facing me like before but bolted when I'd come too far to the side. Pretty much it seemed that he kept his head facing straight, and if I came around far enough to leave the vision of his far eye, that was enough to trigger his flight. I'd let loose the coils as he ran off and he only stopped when a fence interrupted his hurried departure. Once that happened, it was very interesting to me that I could easily put a little feel on the line and he respond with, "Okay...here I am," turn to face me and I could reel him back in with no problem. In fact, I have Dinky to thank for my proficiency in letting coils run out and then winding them back in. He definitely did more to improve my lariat management skills than any equine before or since!

When he was close and standing facing me, I began to use the rope around his neck like a halter rope. I worked on presenting the feel to have him step a front foot to the side. He just couldn't do it at first. He'd step straight forwards or bolt. I hung in there, presented—he was scared and confused—I insisted, and finally, a try! I released and rubbed his nose and just stood there for a few minutes.

Tom uses a 40 foot lariat attached to Dinky's halter to help stay connected to the mule during frequent run offs. *(Dianne Madden)*

It didn't take long before we built on that little start and he was giving me little sideways steps in either direction when I asked. The understanding developed and allowed not only a new move for his repertoire but with it some newfound relaxation—a confidence that when I presented this new feel, there was a definite answer to it. For the first time he also gave a few licks-and-chews, which seemed to confirm some positive feedback from Dinky. Dianne also noticed and commented on this right away.

It's taken two chapters to share only the first one-and-a-half sessions I had with Dinky. The truth is, observing him and then breaking things down to the point that I could find somewhere to start (let alone begin to get him searching, finding some answers, and feeling a little better about things) could fill many more pages than this. Weaving these Dinky Chronicle chapters into this book, I hope, is a way to demonstrate some reality about how a tough horsemanship project like this unfolds—a little at a time, over time, with other things in between.

Breakthroughs, setbacks, and dedicating time and energy to helping horses (or mules) get to feeling better is like this. With Dinky I go do a little, I see what shakes out, I assess things by comparing what I see to what I've learned in my own horsemanship journey, I reflect on what I've learned from Harry that might help, I even bring up Dinky questions at clinics...and the process unfolds over time. Through all this for me, the greatest challenge and the greatest benefit has been getting and keeping Dinky's thought with me. I can't stress enough what a key that is to everything else that unfolds, and I'm profoundly grateful to Harry for that insight when I can manage to keep it *in sight*!

It's exhilarating to get some good changes, and then it's time to work on the next spot. The next step with Dinky was the flag—something as far as the Maddens knew he'd never been introduced to, and a tool I definitely was planning on using if ever I was going to approach those homicidally untrimmable hind feet! And that is a whole other chapter....

Chapter 7

(Tom Moates)

Harry's Definition of Training, The Rest of the Story

I shared an unusual event in the Introduction to *Further Along the Trail*, the previous book in this series. It was when Harry arrived at the discussion table during a clinic at Mendin' Fences Farm in Tennessee with a note pad. On it he had written out his carefully constructed definition of horse training. I, however, neglected to reveal a critical part of that story—the beginning of it—which I want to be sure to share now.

Providing the reason behind his decision to write that definition, even belated like this, puts it into proper context for folks keeping up with the narrative threading through these books. It also provides a great example of the radical differences which can exist in how people think about working with horses and what that might mean for the poor horse. It's also redeeming for me since Harry called me out on this a year later at another Mendin' Fences table talk reminding me that I'd neglected to tell the whole tale in the first place (busted!).

To tell you the truth, by the time *Further Along the Trail* was wrapping up and I was writing the Introduction, I'd simply forgotten about this first part of the discussion. I remembered Harry's definition, though, and was so taken by it and the fact that he'd spent time carefully constructing it to share with us, that I wanted to include it. I dug up my notes from the clinic, and sure enough, there was the verbatim definition scribbled down in the moment, but it didn't include part one of the discussion either. So alas, Harry's definition got described in the Introduction like he'd just showed up to the table with it out of the blue one morning to share with us—which isn't how it happened.

Let me just share part of that Introduction here to be sure you know exactly what was written:

> It was Friday, May 27, 2011. I'm certain of that because it is the only time I ever witnessed horsemanship clinician, Harry Whitney, come to the table for a discussion during a clinic with a notebook in hand to read something he had written down. This being rather unusual, I wrote down exactly what he had written down along with the date in my clinic journal.
>
> A group of maybe a dozen of us sat around a bunch of tables arranged in a rectangle in the middle of the screened-in pavilion at Mendin' Fences Farm in Tennessee. It was the last day of the first week of the annual Tennessee clinics that year. Harry opened up the notebook and read aloud what he had penned:
>
> "Training horses is discovering a communication appropriate for each individual horse whereby we can most agreeably influence their thought to believe that they are desirous to do the very things we know we want to do."
>
> I could never have boiled down Harry's idea of what horsemanship should be—defining what training horses is—to that extent. But since he was able to do so, and I was there to record it, I'm sure going to share it here!

The first part of that story is simply that Harry undertook the exercise to write his definition of horse training as a kind of response to another one brought to his attention earlier during the clinic.

The day before, a long time student of Harry's and regular at the Mendin' Fences Farm clinics for many years, Kathy Baker, handed off a piece of paper to Harry. It was a typed up interview someone

Kathy Baker works Spirit, a Morgan driving horse, on long lines during a clinic in June, 2012 in the new facility at Mendin' Fences Farm in Rogersville, Tennessee. *(Tom Moates)*

had conducted with another horseman which included a definition of training. Who it was isn't important (I didn't recognize him anyway, to be honest), but the point is that he apparently is a successful, professional horseman. Therefore, his definition of training reflects his core beliefs about human/horse interactions.

These must be beliefs that he holds dear. They are, as I see it, the condensed reality of what he sees as existing in the relationship between horse and human. It also is impossible (again, me talking here) to separate one's deep seated horsemanship ideology from one's actions when working with a horse. That's why this horsemanship journey is so difficult if one strives to learn and improve, because to get any real transformation with a horse, one first must change oneself! Like with the horse, first we must grab and redirect our own thoughts before we can make any changes in our presentation, timing, or feel and help our horses.

Kathy reads, blogs, works professionally with horses, and keeps studying the horse constantly, so it's not surprising she would find something like this interview and take note of it. She says she had a question relating to the interview, but it was Harry who latched onto the fellow's definition and felt inspired to write one for himself. I'm guessing that to both Harry and Kathy the definition stood out like a Doberman in a pack of toy Poodles. I'm guessing, too, that it probably got a simple nod from plenty of other readers.

In researching this chapter, naturally I went about looking for that definition to include here. I got in touch with Kathy and it took her a bit of work to put her hands on it—it was a year and a half later—but she did it! So, without any further suspense, the definition that inspired Harry to write his is:

Training horses is discovering the most advantageous leverage counteracting the horse's favorite evasion.

Now, compare to:

Training horses is discovering a communication appropriate for each individual horse whereby we can most agreeably influence their thought to believe that they are desirous to do the very things we know we want to do.

That really doesn't need expounding upon, does it? (Thanks, Harry!)

Chapter 8

(Carol Moates)

Hey, Everybody!

A dear friend recently e-mailed me. She lives out in the wilds of the northwest with her husband, her horses, and her St. Bernards. It was January and she was both sick and snowed in. Like so many of us, regardless of the weather and our own troubles, there are critical chores to do for our four legged companions. On top of recuperating, she just had come in from feeding horses with the temperature at -1F on the mercury when she wrote me.

She began winter with the plan to spend those days when she couldn't be outside riding or doing much with her horses specifically thinking about working with a horse's thoughts. Riding with Harry in recent years really crystallized for her that getting and leading the horse's thought is a cornerstone of getting a horse to feel better about interacting with people. She really wanted to delve deeper into understanding more about working with a horse's thoughts, and

Ross Jacobs, Harry, and Tom discuss critical aspects of horsemanship in Salome, Arizona, in March 2006. *(Michéle Jedlicka)*

with that focus in mind she says she went about watching videos of Tom Dorrance and Ray Hunt, re-reading my books, re-reading *Old Men and Horses* by Ross Jacobs, and reading Ross's blog (www.goodhorsemanship.com.au) in its entirety. She says as she read, compared, and thought about the horse's thought theme, she'd recall specific conversations we had at clinics and emails between us which she dredged up and re-read, as well.

She came across one from me that so grabbed her attention that she re-e-mailed it back to me. It had helped her understand a couple things, and she thought that I might want to share it as an essay somewhere or in an upcoming book. So, I re-read it.

The e-mail had caught one of those moments where things just clicked in my brain. I recognized that in a flash of keystrokes the words to share something important and often hard to describe just came to me in this one. I happened to be working on this book at the time this e-mail made its way back to me, so I considered taking it and making it into an essay chapter. But I think as an e-mail, just as it is, it takes on the task of explaining my understanding of a piece of Harry's horsemanship.

So I will resist the temptation to elaborate on this e-mail in this chapter. To do so would only muddy the waters of this succinct observation. Thanks to my friend, a serious student of the horse, we'll let this be an open e-mail to everybody....

Hey Everybody,

So...I've got to be sure not to step into territory that can't be addressed very well without seeing what's going on with the horse(s) and you.

I don't want to make any mis-assumptions about what you've got going on there even though you describe things extremely well. But perhaps talking a little more about driving might be helpful?

You might already have a similar vision, so this might not be helpful, but I'll just follow the thoughts I've got after reading your last note. Let's take the flag. It has many uses including helping folks get bigger when they're not so big to begin with. It also parallels most anything we might use to approach a horse (hands, ropes, slickers...whatever). Harry (I'd say) first gets a horse feeling good about the flag when he

Harry flags Whisky, a blue roan gelding Derrick Hicks was riding at the 2012 Virginia Bible/horsemanship clinic for his brother, Jeffrey.
(Carol Moates)

goes to use one. He introduces it and makes sure they're familiar with the feel of it and it really becomes an extension of himself. Then, he can use the flag to put an ask in there for something. You might notice that after each ask, Harry typically has folks then rub the horse with the flag—for example: person rubs horse lovingly with flag, person then offers with lead rope for horse to step forward, horse doesn't get it, person whips the flag to put an ask in there, horse steps forward, person should instantly rub horse with the flag as the horse walks off.

But what just happened there? If I was watching Harry do that bit of flagging I'd say it happened like this…Harry has the horse feeling good about him and the flag—not fearful of it. He offers feel on the lead rope to step forward ("beginning where he wants to end up") but the horse doesn't get it. So he changes the *presentation* of himself and the flag.

This is where the rubber meets the road and I think the spot where you're voicing your concern.

Right here, the horse has had every chance to feel the presentation on the rope and respond. Regardless of whether he ignores that or has no idea what it means, it makes no difference, the next step immediately is human-getting-bigger-ness (in our example, putting an ask in the flag). Harry will up the energy in that flag and flap it but it is not directed at the horse's body to drive him in any direction. The flag gets big enough, rather, to say, "Hey! Try something!" Whatever change he gets, that first time I'm guessing Harry would take it and go to rubbing the horse again comfortingly with the flag. He might take a backwards step even if he really wants a forward step because at least the horse isn't still standing there stuck doing nothing. Now, two more tries and Harry might not be accepting that backwards step, but rather than driving him from behind with the flag to get that forward step, Harry will more likely just keep presenting with the flappy flag so the horse tries something else. Eventually, the horse will take a forward step—Harry knows it even if the horse doesn't yet—so the flag helps him to be big enough to keep the search going.

Harry reassures Melissa Hanson's Quarter Horse mare by rubbing her with the flag after introducing it to her during a clinic at FitzFarm in Eagle Lake, Minnesota in July, 2010. *(Tom Moates)*

I think the key element to this is the immediate rubbing of the horse with the flag after getting a change. And, it is most critical because (and I know I've heard Harry say this), you never want the horse to feel he's *fleeing* from it. Fleeing from it equals driving the horse, as far as I'm concerned. Once you have the horse moving off of the flag for a reason of fear, you've planted that seed in there, and while useful to get a quick change in a horse, it does not help establish with-you-ness in the least.

So I might just ask myself, regardless of what I'm doing with my horse at any given moment, am I directing my horse and causing him to squirt away from something to where I want, or, am I doing something big enough that I'm keeping him searching but not squeezing him into the confined box of my desired outcome? Of course, (maybe this is part of what you're feeling, I don't know?) there can, and probably will be, flee in getting big enough to cause a horse to break his thought loose, especially at first—that's why it is best to immediately get right to him with rubbing the flag (or whatever)—he must not become afraid of the thing getting bigger but must understand it is a request from you for him to start seeking an answer…and right now. Consistent handling of this means the horse will develop the understanding that he need never be afraid of your getting bigger but that it has a specific meaning, that he needs to let go of whatever thought he has right then and seek out what you're asking. Once he knows there always, always, is an answer involved in an ask then he knows he has absolutely zero need to be worried about your biggerness, and in fact should relax into your firmness. This ought to even get right into the reins when you ride, etc.

Woops...looks like I just about wrote a chapter there! Sorry, it just slipped out. And I could be totally out in left field from what you were thinking about anyway.

Guess I better get to town. Have fun!

Tom

Chapter 9

(Tom Moates)

Travels with Harry

The windshield on Harry's RV is enormous. Like a big fish eye lens, it provided a portal through the otherwise enclosed interior of the coach revealing a panoramic view of the world as we began in earnest our journey west. From the galley, back at about mid-ship, looking forward at the brilliant morning splendor spilling in through the windshield was like standing inside a big box camera with the shutter open. I felt like the film!

I swayed my way up to the front, bracing against furniture as I went. We were barreling along Interstate 90 west of Sioux Falls, South Dakota. We'd gotten this far from Eagle Lake, Minnesota the night before and shut the rig down for the night in a truck stop parking lot. It was a good launching point for this dawning day which had a couple stops scheduled and would need to end in Wyoming for us to keep on track to the next clinic.

There's no engine or hood out in front on Harry's motor home, so where the windshield ends the road begins. I could see straight down to the pavement as it rolled under the bumper to become part of the distance behind us. I stood in the stairwell by the passenger seat with my elbows on the dash feeling like I was leaning forward off the bow of a ship right out over the water as we cruised. Harry sat, as he must for so many hours and days each year, in the driver's seat, hands gripping the large steering wheel and looking out at the traffic and surroundings. He's come this way so many times before that he makes comparisons to previous years—this was a dry one, he said.

I gazed out at two gray ribbons of highway that led clear to where the horizon met the blue sky. It was not my familiar Virginia horizon either, just some few miles distant (seeming a long ways off when forests don't block the view), but a South Dakota horizon, so far off that countless square miles of sunflower fields blooming golden between here and there even seemed small in the bigness. Instead of feeling just flat, however, to me it seemed the curvature of the earth was perceptible in the openness—that the spherical shape of the planet's surface actually caused the land in all directions to eventually dip out of view. It was a strange sensation for this traveler.

The day was young, about seven in the morning. It was our first full day of travel, August 1st, 2012. Harry was seat-belted in his cockpit, piloting the big diesel RV down the road. I stood in front of the passenger's seat, camera in hand with my head up by the

The world's biggest sculpted bull head. *(Tom Moates)*

glass, just soaking in the bigness of the scene unfurling before me and snapping photos nearly nonstop. To me it was all so new that everything seemed photo worthy—grain elevators in the distance, enormous wind generators in the distance, a herd of horses in the distance, the world's biggest metal sculpted bull's head in the distance (everything was in the distance, and yet still perfectly visible).

The chance for this trip opened up earlier in the year when I got the bright idea to see if I could talk Harry into letting me tag along to a couple of his annual clinics that summer. Of course, I strive to get to Harry's clinics anytime and anywhere, so that aspect was awesome in itself. This time, however, I'd be spending two weeks with him in the RV, which would include driving across 1500 miles of America I'd never seen before, as well!

Leaving home is always tricky for me because we have a farm and animals. Summer, however, is usually the best time for me to try and travel. Most of our horses are on pasture then, so there are just a couple that need feeding each day. We heat the house with firewood, thus summer relieves the added burden of dealing with that. We have a sizable garden and put up a ton of food each season, which makes for some very busy spells, but Carol manages that enterprise, and the timing for this trip wasn't horrible for any harvesting. She encouraged me to go, so I made some calls, bought some airline tickets, and soon I was on a flight to Minnesota.

Suzy Fitzsimmons had invited me out to Harry's clinic at her place in Eagle Lake, Minnesota back in the summer of 2010, which had been fantastic. She had been encouraging me to make it out again, so I flew into Minneapolis where she picked me up from the airport and drove me back to her farm. Due to some family obligations earlier that week, I only caught the last couple of days of the FitzFarm clinics. But I was there long enough to see a ton of friends made on the earlier trip, see two full days of riding, and sign a bunch of books for folks.

At the end of the final day of the FitzFarm clinic, Harry and I packed up his stuff and we hit the road by about six o'clock that evening. Of course, Harry has made this general circuit of America going on two decades now, so he knows the ropes. Things like not stopping at night ahead of a city to be stuck in morning

Harry, spending time as he so often must, driving his RV across America to the next clinic—here we are in the Badlands of South Dakota.
(Tom Moates)

rush hour traffic the next day are well entrenched in his mental operational manual. Not driving after dark is another one. We split the difference that first night and made a couple hundred miles getting to the other side of Sioux Falls after dark. Now we were en route to another long time clinic destination of Harry's, Stevensville, Montana.

Eagle Lake to Stevensville is 1200 miles. That means Harry has to leave out of Minnesota, drive completely across South Dakota, cut across a corner of Wyoming, and go nearly the entire length of Montana to get to the next job. As I mentioned, it was August 1st, and Harry's Stevensville clinic would begin bright and early on the morning of August 4th. Three days to get there, get set up, and get a little rest—three days for 1200 miles.

On this leg of his annual trip Harry tries to get into Stevensville a day early to park the RV at the home of some friends and spend the day decompressing. That's what we were shooting for. It allows at least one day to visit a little with old friends, take a few pictures, get a haircut, make calls, pretty much anything that needs doing for the next week since once clinic starts, it is hard for him to find time to even make a call during business hours.

Another thing that occurred to me is that when you have to cover 1200 miles in three days, it doesn't leave much room for trouble—and this was just one leg of many on this North American circuit of Harry's. It's no wonder he makes a Herculean effort to keep the motor home up on maintenance. It's a terrible thought, but it occurred to me what a disaster it would be for everybody if the clinician is late for a clinic by a day or more. Preparation for these clinics are made months in advance, and folks and their horses are going to be at a host place for only a few set days. It is a big commitment for people to sign up, get there with horses, take vacation from work, and so forth, and Harry takes that seriously. He also needs a paycheck to pay for all this running around. I easily saw why he'd want a big, quality diesel machine (the RV reminded me of a road tractor, really) to cover the distances and geographies he must each year and do all he can to keep on target with his schedule.

It was our first day on the road and I'd already done my part to complicate Harry's schedule. From studying a map of our potential trip earlier that year, I'd realized we were going to be rolling through the Black Hills later that day. I arranged for us to take a detour south of I-90 down near Custer to a ranch in a little place called Pringle and meet Amy Kirk.

Amy is a rancher and writes a newspaper column and blog called, *A Ranchwife's Slant: Cowboys, Kids, and Ranch Life* (www.AmyKirk.com). I'd lined up an interview with Amy for *Western Horseman* magazine and got Harry the job of taking photos for the story. I also had negotiated with Amy to publish her first book, a compilation of her columns with the same title as the blog. It would be the first non-Tom Moates book for the Spinning Sevens Press, and I was eager to get the chance to meet her and see the setting for many of her great essays. It looked like we'd be able to swing down to her ranch, do the interview and photo shoot, and have a meeting about her upcoming book, then get back on the road and over into Wyoming before the end of the day if all went well.

Harry kept the RV in the wind and we flew across South Dakota. I was just mesmerized at the changing scenes through the windshield and took a million pictures through the bug squish. Late morning we gained an hour by crossing out of Central Time into Mountain Time. By around 11:00 a.m., Harry pointed out some particularly peculiar landscape ahead—it was the Badlands. He offered to detour through Badlands National Park, and I jumped at the chance!

It was absolutely incredible. White formations of I'm-not-sure-what (not really soil, not really clay, not really sand…it was some weird combination of them all, and felt like it, too) surrounded us. It was a landscape clearly tortured by eons of wind and torrential downpours. The colors became more spectacular as we ventured around. Stripes of red and rust colored material ran horizontally in many of the hills, spires, pyramids, and pinnacles. Some sloughing buttes and hillsides towered like monuments or castle walls. Other times we'd be on flat ground that just suddenly dropped off into a crazy maze of eroded arroyos that was sort of like looking into a mini-Grand Canyon.

Honestly, you just have to look at photos to get any kind of idea of what the Badlands are like. They defy description. I can sure see why banditos and rustlers would want to hole up in there, like they were reputed to have done back in the old west—good luck on finding anybody in there that wanted to stay hidden!

It took at least a couple of hours to wind through the Badlands. Once on the other side of them, we continued west for the Black Hills. The Sturgis motorcycle rally was going on at about this time, so Harley Davidsons were everywhere. Little towns nestled in valleys we'd pass through had streets lined with parked sparkling chrome machines.

It was a year of quite severe drought through the mid-west

The Badlands of South Dakota. *(Tom Moates)*

and wildfires raged in many states. We began to see the evidence. Smoke would come in like a fog, and sometimes visibility would drop to less than a mile on the Interstate. Charred remains of forest could be seen as we drove deeper into the hills.

Just as evident as fire damage was the huge number of dead standing trees. Hillsides of green pines would show sometimes as much as 50% brown, dead pines still standing scattered among the living. It was the work of an evil weevil...the pine beetle, to be accurate. It left me wondering what the majestic mountains would be like if they lost all their green pine robes and became just naked hills?

Tom interviews Amy Kirk for a *Western Horseman* article. *(Harry Whitney)*

We made it to the Kirk Ranch, noticing that they recently suffered a near miss with a wildfire which had scorched the forest almost within sight of their home. Pulling up we knew we were in the right place since, the roof of a nice red barn announced it with the ranch's brand, K over CC, in big white letters. Harry drove over the cattle guard into the place and we met Amy's husband, Art, and teenage son, Myles. They were about to head out for a fencing project.

Harry and I piled into a car with them and they drove us back up the road to meet Amy at a special old wooden barn. It had been built by Art's ancestors and was the spot where he and Amy had been married. Amy and I sat in the shade inside the barn and did the interview while Harry moseyed around—I could hear the click, click, click of his camera shutter even when he was out of view. Then Harry did a shoot of Amy for the magazine with the barn as a backdrop, and we rode back to the home place to meet her daughter, Renee, her dog, Pepper, and check out Art's shop. Then we climbed back aboard the RV.

Heading out the cattle guard, we couldn't help but stop again. The Kirks have an antique threshing machine setting on a hill by the side of the road. I had seen many of these parked along the way that day, but this one was uncommon because it was set up as if it were running. All the augers were extended and two old wooden wagons were set in place like it was in action. Harry loves photographing old cars, trucks, tractors, and machines so he went to town on this rig!

The Kirk's antique threshing machine set up by the road in one of their pastures. *(Tom Moates)*

Then it was back on the road. We got to Custer and headed west on route 16. It was after 7:00 o'clock when we hit the Wyoming border. Highway 16 takes a diagonal, northwesterly track that meets up again with Interstate 90 at a town called Moorcroft. We hopped on the Interstate there and got as far as Gillette before calling it a night. My first day on the road with Harry had been amazing, but it seemed like four days were crammed in there!

It was hard to believe that just the day before our journey began Harry had taught a full day of clinic. We'd traveled the length of South Dakota making over 500 miles, not to mention all the amazing things I'd seen and the stops we'd made, and we still were less than halfway to the next clinic destination. Tomorrow we'd have to make some swift miles to get to Stevensville with daylight left. That night we found another parking lot with RV friendly parking policies and got some sleep. What an adventure!

Dawn broke. The sunlight streamed across hilly pasture land now, and soon we were rolling again up Interstate 90. Before long, we passed through Sheridan, Wyoming heading northeast to the Montana border. When we got to the state line, Harry pulled over and I jumped out and ran under the Welcome to Montana sign,

Tom acting like a tourist at the South Dakota/Montana border. *(Harry Whitney)*

stepping a foot for the first time in the state, and acting like a total tourist. Harry snapped a few photos of me by the sign for posterity (and Facebook).

This wasn't a day for many stops—we were bucketing down the Interstate just making time towards our final destination. The diesel purred along and the pavement alternated from really smooth to regular, repetitious dips at times. The miles swooshed by a hundred at a time, and I was still at the windshield snapping photos of everything as we sped along. The openness I'd first seen in South Dakota continued, and maybe even amplified in Montana, if that's possible. Such vistas!

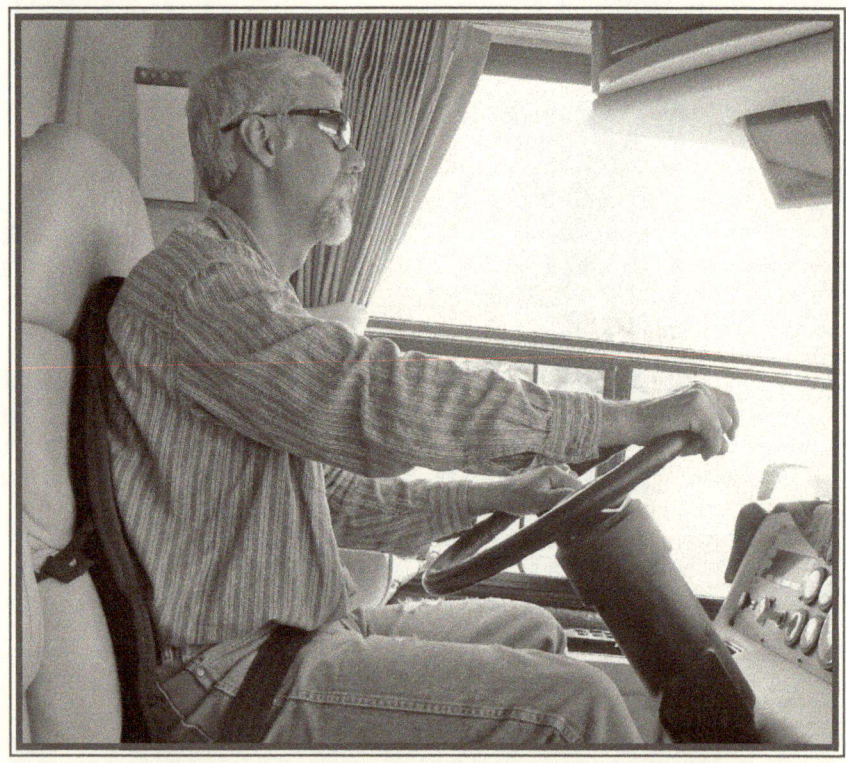

Tom finds another way to drive Harry crazy somewhere in Montana.
(Harry Whitney)

We passed through the Crow Indian Reservation, which, lucky for them, still showed some signs of green in the fields. The further we traveled west, however, the more brown and burnt the landscape became. Irrigated fields along rivers were a stark deep green in contrast to the baked soil and bleached broom straw looking remnants of plants scattered everywhere else.

We passed through Billings, Livingston, and Butte. I drove for awhile and Harry caught a power nap in the passenger seat. The stretch of highway I got to drive happened to be one with a long section that wound through a sharp pass with wicked cross winds—it had warning signs and wind socks along the edge of the road to prove it—and it was a windy day! I did manage to hold that big machine mostly between the navigational lines, but in the strong wind it was a lot like piloting a bread box on a kid's Matchbox car track in a hurricane.

A fire had been started on one stretch of highway we came across. The flames were shooting skyward right off the edge of the other lane of highway from where we were passing, and emergency crews were just arriving. We passed and could see a truck with blown tires on one side. We figured with the dry conditions, sparks from the rims on the highway had started the blaze. Throughout the day smoke from the big wildfires, most of which were hundreds of miles distant, occasionally darkened the sky and wafted in and out of our path.

In the late afternoon we reached Missoula. There we got off the Interstate and set a southerly course on Highway 93 for Stevensville. Soon we were traveling along a plush valley. Harry explained this was the Bitterroot Valley. It was an amazing green oasis compared to the land we'd been passing through. The Bitterroot Range, with its sharp, bare rock faces, towered to the west. A smaller range, the Sapphire Mountains, defined the valley more humbly to the east.

We made it to Harry's friends' place well before dark. Harry knew the drill and backed the motor home into its regular yearly spot. Central to everything was a log cabin home complete with dogs in a fenced yard and a canopy of big trees shading the whole area around the house, driveway, yard, and several out buildings. It was really pleasant, and standing back on *terra firma* after 700 miles of riding was nice, too.

A view of the round pen and pasture with the Bitteroot Mountains in the background taken from inside the barn during the 2012 clinic at Kootenai Equestrian Center in Stevensville, Montana. *(Tom Moates)*

Harry and I got to visit with these folks that evening and the next day until early afternoon. Then he fired up the RV again and we headed just a short distance over to Malika Coston's place, Kootenai Creek Equestrian Center, where the clinic would be held. The driveway was draped with trees and branches for about a quarter mile, and I haven't heard Harry fuss about trees like that since he drove into our place back in Virginia! Harry is not a fan of trees to begin with, but when they're rubbing down the sides and roof of his RV, he gets downright testy about it!

It seems odd not to jump into a horsemanship clinic discussion right here—especially since it was a great one and I took notes enough to fill up a third of a composition book—but, like with Harry's schedule, I need to keep this story about our travels moving along if I'm going to get to the next stop.

The clinic was fantastic, though, with many folks and horses there that I'd met the year before at Harry's place in Salome, and many new friends I met for the first time. I'm certain that having so many friendly folks at all of these stops is a large part of what keeps Harry going strong. Wherever I've attended his clinics, people are always excited to see him and eager to be friendly and help out if he needs anything. This big extended family has to make life on the road much more bearable.

Also notable for me at the Montana clinic was that Malika surprised me and asked if I'd give a book reading one evening when they had a dinner for everyone in the barn. I did it, and it was the first (and as yet, the only) time I've given a book reading. Luckily, the audience wasn't overly prone to heckling and the material I chose on the spur of the moment got some laughs.

The end of a clinic is always a little sad and exciting, both. I'm eager to go home and put to the test some things I've picked up, and I'm always sorry to part from Harry and other friends, especially where I've been present for the whole clinic week. Clinics are little worlds unto themselves, and there can be some wonderful changes in people and horses during them. When it ends, reality rushes back in on you like the end of a movie that's so good you actually forgot you were in the theater until the credits start rolling and the house lights come up.

The Montana clinic wrapped up and Harry had a couple of days to get 400 miles over to Wenatchee, Washington to his regular clinics there hosted by Elayne Hovde. Just past half way, Harry's route passes through Spokane, Washington. Being a sizable city, I'd arranged for my flight home out of the airport there. We loaded up most everything the evening after the clinic ended. The next morning we pulled the RV's shore power, got a few things stowed for travel, and pushed our way back out through the branches along the driveway and headed north to Missoula.

Before long, we were back on Interstate 90 again, heading west. We weren't really crunched for time on this leg of the trip since we could make Spokane by nightfall easily, but he did have a late afternoon chiropractors appointment in the city that day. Harry has pretty severe neck troubles and part of his annual travels around the country includes stops with certain chiropractors for adjustments, which he is able to work into his schedule as he passes through.

Harry was hoping to get some photos of Bison, too, so we detoured north off of I-90 and went into the National Bison Range in Dixon, Montana. We were able to watch a huge herd on an open plain there, but they were quite a ways in the distance, so the photos weren't spectacular.

We looped back down to the Interstate and headed for Idaho. The mountains when we crossed the state line were phenomenal! The vantage point looked out over an immense valley with rolling peaks beyond it. These mountains were carpeted with healthy evergreens, thousands of acres of them for as far as I could see.

The other thing about Idaho that stood out in my mind is that the Cabella's store in Post Falls has a complimentary customer round pen in the parking lot for shoppers to corral their horses while

A courtesy round pen in the Cabella's parking lot in Post Falls, Idaho.
(Tom Moates)

they shop. (I've heard this is a regular Cabella's feature.) I had to take a photo of that! I figure it is to give horses a break from their trailers, not to provide a corral for cowboys who ride into town for provisions—but I could be wrong.

Harry had introduced me to my first Cabella's experience in Minnesota back in 2010. I had been amazed at the museum of natural history it had taxidermized inside! Truly amazing, and whenever Harry and I manage to get around one now we stop in. We had lunch at this one and hit the bargain cave in the back of the store, of course. (Harry got a heavy, down insulated coat...he was freezing in the store and so he found a deal and wore it around while we shopped, and then paid for it while still wearing it—he was still wearing it the last time I saw him in Arizona months later, come to think of it.)

From Post Falls, it wasn't far to Spokane. Spokane is a real city, and while Harry maneuvered the big RV with expert skill, the traffic was typically congested. We wove in and out of lanes, made our way through the streets of downtown, and got parked by the building we needed to get to for his chiropractors appointment.

Afterwards, we drove into increasingly rush hour traffic and headed in the direction of the airport. I didn't fly until the next morning, but we figured we'd find a place where we could overnight the RV and then find some supper. We got lucky, and Elayne (whom I met in Salome, Arizona at a clinic in 2011 and was the host of his next clinic, mentioned above) was around Spokane that afternoon, so she met us and we had supper together and visited for a couple hours that evening.

Then another day was done. Harry dropped me off early at

the airport the next morning after we grabbed a fast food breakfast and tied up some loose ends. I made it all the way to Denver before getting stuck with cancelled flights and all that nonsense. I have to say, I honestly could have gone right on down the road some more with Harry. For every horsemanship question I seem to get answered, two more sprout out. I'm seeing more of Harry's teachings at work in myself and others than ever before, but it just exposes to me how much I still don't know. Even with the brutal schedule, I'd happily make the whole circuit with Harry to learn all I could.

This chapter gives just a slight insight into the world Harry lives in while on the road. To tell you the truth, when he's at home in Salome, Arizona, with back-to-back clinics, it isn't any better—sometimes it's worse! Harry lives a spiraling life with a momentum of its own that seems to drag him along with it, all so that folks like me can try and gain some insights into getting better with our horses. I'm not entirely sure why he does it, but I'm sure glad he does! It has, however, provided him with more than a couple decades of relative chaos.

Even with the highlights of our trip hit on here, so many details are omitted because the days were just vibrating full of all kinds of things start to finish. It is impossible to depict it accurately—there's just too much stuff—and I was with Harry for only two weeks. One of the main impressions I took away from my travels with Harry is a profound appreciation of how he juggles so much as he rolls along. Whole days disappear. Time warps in mysterious ways. Weeks melt away into a blob. Good luck on keeping track of much outside of where you need to get to today to be where you need to be tomorrow—and don't forget to eat! Or fuel up where you can! Or call about that insurance thing while the office is open on a weekday during office hours Arizona time! Or sign and send out some photos folks have paid for. Or call about some issue with a clinic two stops ahead, which will be today before you know it. Trying to do any regular thing in a life with such irregularity is more than a little challenging.

One example from the trip which really stood out for me shows just how hard it is for Harry to get anything done. One of the magazines I contribute to, *Ranch & Reata* (www.ranchandreata.com), lined up a large spread of 20 of Harry's photos (which ran in the October/November 2012 issue). The photos already were chosen and we needed to provide captions, which I was typing up for him. Harry and I had gone over some of these on the phone already, but we still needed to review what we had done and complete the final third of them. I had everything set up to take care of this when I left Virginia in my notebook and laptop. I figured, two weeks together... no problem, we'll get that done one evening, or on the road while we're rolling along. Right!

It never happened. We thought about it a couple times along the way, but there honestly was never a moment to do it. Either we were too tuckered to think straight in the evenings (not conducive to good writing), or we were going, eating, stopping for a moment, meeting someone, clinicking, or in a push to get something else done critical to the operation at hand. Finally, we were in the airport parking lot, up early before I had to go catch my flight home, both tired and not wanting to do this, but knowing we'd better get it done, and doing it. It was arduous and unfun. Then we still worked on it over the phone that day as I was stuck in airports and he was driving to Wenatchee, but we got it completed. I think that's what Harry often has to do—just stop everything, block it all out, and focus on one highly pressing matter before going about the rest of his day again.

Those two weeks were a whirlwind. It was awesome and amazing, but it was a blur—and I came to realize it's the way life is on the road with Harry. Making miles, snapping a few photos here and there for his own enjoyment, catching up with a friend or two when the timing works out...that's about all there's time for giving the tight schedule to get from one clinic to the next. Then he arrives at a clinic spot where naturally his presence is much anticipated, so the buzz of clinic life begins and carries on with its own amazing momentum, and then it's over and he packs up and gets on the road with only so much time to get to the next one....

Chapter 10

(Dianne Madden)

Flagging Dinky
(The Dinky Chronicles, Part Three)

There's a distinctive sound a bullet makes when it passes you. If you've ever been somewhat down range of a rifle shot you probably noticed that it makes a kind of *Snap!* (You don't necessarily need to be shot at to hear this, but it increases the odds that you've noticed it.) I've been told that sound is the bullet breaking the sound barrier. I'm sure I heard that same sonic snap as Dinky's hind hoof grazed the fabric on the arm of my ranch coat before it went *Whack!* into a fence board. Yep, I'm thinking that mule kick actually broke the sound barrier. A couple inches closer and it might have broken my arm, too!

As you might imagine from Dinky's earlier introduction, I avoided directly reaching for his hind feet the first couple of times I worked with him. On the contrary, I spent time just trying to establish basic communication with Dinky to get him feeling better about being handled in general. My hope was to gradually work towards those back feet and pick them up with as little distress to the mule (and myself!) as possible.

Working with Mister Dinky the Mule in general was going great considering how much anxiety for humans he packed around. I continued with the 40 foot lariat looped around his neck for awhile. Still, we frequently hit spots where something became too much for him and he had to blast away from me. Out would go the coils until he stopped by the fence only to turn back and get reeled in again.

But progress was being made. I worked on establishing what different feels on the line meant, getting some consistency of handling going, and probably for the first time in his life proving that there are dependable answers he can find to "asks" from a human. Once he was able to step his front feet laterally a little when asked without needing to leave town, I decided to see how things would go with introducing him to the flag.

The Maddens hired me mainly to see if I could help Dinky get to the point that he could be trimmed without being a danger to himself and others. This was essential to them regarding his ongoing care, so it was a major consideration in how I chose to proceed with things. I'd need to address those back feet soon and get him feeling better about having a human messing with them. Luckily, Dianne and Pat understood that it was going to take some time to sort out those homicidally untrimmable hind feet and that all these other spots of trouble in Dinky I'd been working on related to that goal as well.

There was no question that I'd be keeping what safe distance I could when approaching the hind-end danger zone. I knew I'd be using a flag to start this process. Introducing the flag to Dinky—

Tom works on getting Dinky to bend through his body when circling. (*Dianne Madden*)

the reigning king of the 180 degree, seeya!, I'm outa here muley maneuvers—went remarkably well.

Dinky was not afraid of the flag itself, which I found to be odd in a good way since he is a mule known for his tremendous trepidation. I guessed most likely he had never seen one, so there were no negative experiences for him to reference like he had with ropes and people's hands. The way he sniffed at the flag and remained mentally present to check it out from the very beginning also revealed he retained some curiosity, which was a delight to see in such a distressed mule.

Playing with the flag quickly corroborated more pieces of the Dinky puzzle I'd been noticing while working him on line. Surprisingly he almost immediately was fine to feel the flag on his nose, face, down his neck, and even down part way along his top line. He was, however, terrified of bending or allowing me to move down along either of his sides much at all. The flag, however, seemed to help get a quick improvement with touching him more and more places on his body.

I just kept playing with this, pushing into troubled territory with the flag but trying to back off before he felt the need to bolt, then going back to trouble spots again, and so on. Soon it was shaping up to the point that he let me move a step or two down his sides to flag him further back on his body. He finally settled into having the flag rubbing him all over except for his hind legs. I even got to his belly, croup, between his hind legs by his sheath, and on the outside of the uppermost part of his backside (but not as low as the stifles) before calling it a day on that initial flagging session.

Still, he was unable to give me any bend in his body without bolting, flag or no flag. If I asked him to tip his thought in a direction, he was able to do that by moving his big round eyes. But, if I asked him to take that thought further to the side to the extent he needed to bring his head around too (thus bending his neck even a little) forget it! He'd leave town before bending. The Maddens and I, however, were amazed to see such promising progress as touching Dinky over most of his body with the flag.

"Dinky Days" became my name for Wednesdays since that was the regular weekday I went out to work with Dinky. I was able to make it to the Maddens' many weeks during the summer and fall. As things progressed, after beginning to work with the flag, I changed from using the lariat looped around his neck and instead clipped the rope to his halter. Having a 40 foot lead rope on a halter allowed me to present to him the feel of working with his standard equipment on his head while still being able to bring him back easily during spooked spells.

Increasingly I was able to get ahead of Dinky's bolting. I'd put the brakes on, turn him back to me, and settle him before he got completely turned 180 degrees away and hopelessly gone to the fence. I noticed that if his thought to flee could be interrupted, the mule seemed just fine to come right back and pick up where we left off.

He has such a hair trigger—mind gone/mind here—it is amazing how quickly and completely he swings from one to the other and perhaps back again in a couple of seconds. To be more accurate I should report that the hair trigger actually is a three stage switch: mind here/mind gone inside himself while standing there shutdown/ mind gone with his body physically leaving at a high rate of speed after it.

Dianne had been picking up Dinky's front feet before I came out the first time. I kept building on that nice start and soon was making a point to pick them out and eventually even rasp on them each time I visited. Those fronts got so good I'd say they were picture perfect by about the fifth session. In fact, I know a few horses around here (who shall remain nameless to protect the guilty) that I wish would get that relaxed and willing to have their front feet trimmed! I kept thinking that if it is possible for Dinky to get that good with his fronts, surely there's hope for the backs.

As time went on I began working Dinky in the little rectangular area between the uphill end of the barn and the fence

Dinky improved tremendously with having his front feet handled, and here Tom works with having him put them on a stand for the first time.
(Dianne Madden)

mentioned in an earlier chapter. He was far less apt to do the 180 degree dance when we were in those close confines. Since the small space kept him from running off, it allowed me the luxury of really asking things in a bigger way to get his thoughts with me and get some better changes.

There began to be a readiness in Dinky to step to either side, come forward, or back when I asked on the lead line. Eventually he began to bend to some extent through his neck and into his body. This progress soon allowed me to bring his thought around to a side far enough that his hindquarters stepped over the opposite way. Soon I even was able to ask him to go out and circle me in either direction with decent success. I was thrilled to see Dinky start to believe that some things can be okay with a human and begin building a whole new understanding from our growing moments of with-you-ness!

Dianne also got hands-on with Dinky and began playing with some of these things as I coached her. I saw many great changes in the mule. The most profound positive transformations, however, were the ones I didn't see. Dianne and Pat had to tell me about these which were differences in Dinky's day-to-day life. When I'd show up for a Dinky Day they often greeted me with, "Guess what!"

Of course curious, I'd say, "What?"

And they'd excitedly explain the various changes they were noticing in Dinky's regular life. (Dinky certainly didn't lack love and caring from his humans who always saw past his problems!) One thing that really stood out for me was when they described how each morning Pat walks their dogs down the main lane which leads straight out in front of their farmhouse between two pastures. For two years Dinky avoided them during this ritual and remained way over at the other end of the field mostly behind the barn. Recently, however, he'd started taking an interest in Pat and company when they walked. Now the mule was coming all the way over to greet them in the morning and even walking along the fence with them sometimes.

"When Dinky started to feel better about himself and started walking over to the fence," Dianne told me, "he also let Pat start rubbing his face and neck. That was a big deal. Before that he didn't like us touching him at all."

That news was the best reward I could imagine for the time we were putting in with Dinky. Hearing that the little fellow was not just better to work with under halter, but feeling good enough inside himself to let down and want to be around people while loose in the pasture was huge.

But there still remained the big sticking point of those hind feet. When I mentioned earlier about the kick which grazed my arm and broke the sound barrier, I wasn't kidding! I've never seen an equine go from zero to full blown battering ram with such blinding speed. I credit Dinky for not killing me, though. I think that kick (and a few others that followed) could have taken me out if he'd chosen to do it. I was being very careful, for sure, but Dinky made no mistakes of aim and I can't take credit for being mentally or physically ahead of him when approaching those hind hooves.

Although I can't be certain what goes on in a mule's mind, I believe Dinky wanted to feel better about things. It really felt like he was starting to meet me halfway in our work. Already he had let down in so many ways. However, that kick was putting me on notice that—under no uncertain terms—putting a hand on his lower legs was over the line and into no-go territory.

What interested me so much about my near-whacked experience was that now for Dinky it wasn't simply about having his lower hind legs touched—rather it was only when they were touched by a hand that he got aggressively protective about them. I'd been playing with the flag on Dinky for several sessions at this point and not only was I able to rub the streamers over much of his body, but I could rub him with my hands along his back, sides, and belly. With the flag, I was able to work all around his hind legs and feet now, usually without much visible trouble. I even could tap each lower leg with the flag and have him relax it and cock it on the toe—a relaxed leg posture Harry had shown me on Festus at a clinic a few years earlier. It was one example of many where my clinic experiences with Harry played a direct role in helping me help Dinky.

Harry, when working on a foot like this, likes to get a horse resting a leg on the toe so he can pick it up without resistance. Again, establishing this has to do with getting a horse's thought with you. If you are working on picking up a foot and the horse has the leg tensed then he is thinking elsewhere, making plans to leave and taking that foot with him, or thinking actively that he doesn't want you messing with it. To relax the foot on the toe when you ask shows his thought is present, focused, and that he is resting the leg easy when you approach it. That is the kind of willingness Harry likes to build in all his interactions with horses.

Another thing I did to safely work on this was use a rope on those hind feet. My lariat has a ring instead of a honda and it provides a very quick release when I let off pressure on the line. I laid a loop on the ground and had Dinky step a hind foot into it, then

Tom roped a hind foot and pulled it forward working to help get Dinky to relax it, then was able to safely hold it forward by the hoof with his hand.
(Dianne Madden)

took the slack up roping it. I worked for awhile putting pressure on the rope and then releasing when he relaxed the leg. I got both sides pretty good with this and soon had him not just relaxing the legs but setting those toes on the ground, too.

I talked to Harry on the phone between Dinky Days when I could. I explained what progress I was seeing with the flag and the rope on the hind feet but explained that whenever I involved my hand on his legs that he knew the difference and was kicking something fierce! Harry suggested taking one of my work gloves, stuffing it with something to make it hand-like, and then putting it on the end of the flag and working on the hind legs and feet with it. Then, when that gets going pretty well, put the glove on my hand and with the hind foot roped, use a combination of rope holding and hand touching to see if I could safely get the hind legs handled once and for all.

It was brilliant! (Why didn't I think of that?) The next time out I put our rope halter on him and then did what Harry suggested—I took one of my work gloves and stuffed it on the end of my flag with all the streamers inside which really made it look like a human hand. Then I approached Dinky with it as I would introduce a flag. He was fine with it on his head, back, sides, and front legs. In fact, by running it down either front leg he would relax the leg like I was using my real hand. On the rump and down the leg, he would tense up. As I went below the stifles, out came the blisteringly fast kicks.

Tom introduces the glove on the end of his flag to Dinky's hind leg.
(Dianne Madden)

Tom works lower down the leg with the glove. *(Dianne Madden)*

I persisted, since my body was safely out of range, and watched the crash-test-dummy-hand take a brutal pounding. With a little time and determination, especially through episodes of kicking the faux hand, he got better about it. Finally, he gave up the kicking for the most part. Then I gave him a break from that and switched things up and went back to using the rope to ask for relaxation.

Next I used the rope to lift the hind feet one at a time up and forward. It went pretty well. Before long he was relaxing those legs as I held them up that way. Then I got the glove/flag and while holding a leg up and forward I rubbed the leg with it. I began choking up on the flag towards the glove with my real hand while moving myself closer to his hind end. Finally, I switched the glove off the end of the flag, put it on my hand, and was able to run it along the rope to the foot and finally was able to rub him with my real hand. Before it was over, I was able to hold both feet up and forward with my hand and let go of the rope. I got bolder, got my trimming tools handy, and then picked them out and even rasped on the toes and sides. It went great!

Of course, having the back feet pulled forward isn't really an arrangement that lends itself to trimming since you can't see what is going on underneath the hoof. I'd need to get those feet pulled out behind him for that. I looped a long halter rope around a fence

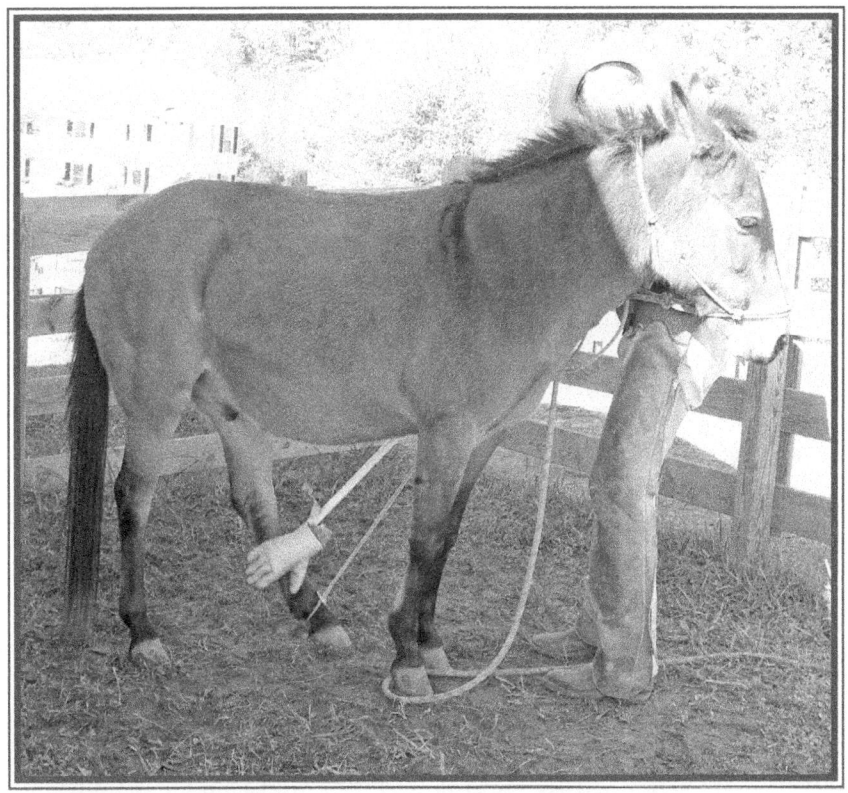

Tom worked both back legs with the fake hand. *(Dianne Madden)*

post so I could hold it from behind Dinky and feed some slack if necessary. Then taking the lariat with a hind foot roped, I began working to lift a hind leg up and backwards with me standing behind him at a distance.

It didn't go great at first. This new situation really bothered him, and I worked both sides with similar results. I worked at this awhile to get him somewhat better about it but never got the worry and kicking relaxed out of him that day.

The big moment when Tom was able to hold Dinky's hind foot out behind him. *(Dianne Madden)*

On October 24, 2012 I wrote in my horsemanship journal, "Big Day for Dinky!" Maybe it should have read, "Big day for Tom!," since I was totally delighted at this monumental moment, and perhaps Dinky didn't register quite the same enthusiasm.

I jotted down the reason for my excitement: "I finally got Dinky's feet not only picked up out back behind him, but also picked out, wire brushed clean, and nipped off! It was awesome! Such an amazing thing to have started with this terribly troubled mule so many months ago now, and to have helped bring him around to such a profoundly positive change!"

On Dinky Day the week before, Diane and Pat told me that they had scheduled their farrier to come out on October 25th to see about trimming the mule. They were hoping this session being on the day before attempting to have Dinky trimmed again would finally allow for success. Their anxiety was understandable, especially since this farrier, who regularly came to care for their Walking Horse, Rowdy, already had sworn off trying to trim Dinky long ago.

Working with Dinky that day, I really just approached things like the previous ones. I did some ground work and then used the flag, the glove on the flag, and ropes on the hind feet both forwards and from behind. I think the relationship and communication between us had built to the point that finally I was confident and able to take a hold of those back hooves and lift them out behind Dinky and let him feel the trimming tools touch them. It was just profound for me to finally get there.

The next day Dianne called as soon as the farrier had left to give me the update. I asked her to e-mail me the details, too. I think she does a great job of both summarizing the history of Dinky's life

Tom finally is able to hold Dinky's hind feet, pick them out, and use the nippers on them. *(Dianne Madden)*

while living with them and describing how things unfolded with the trimming that day. So I'll just let her tell this part of the story and share her e-mail here.

Hi Tom,

I went back in my mind to when we first brought Dinky to live with us and this is what I remember.

The first time we tried to have Dinky trimmed was when my vet came to give him his vaccinations. They wouldn't come out until we could get Dinky in a halter. I had not been able to halter him no matter how hard I tried. My vet recommended I find a trainer. I happened to meet a lady that has several mules and she recommended a mule trainer she used.

He came and got the halter on by twisting Dinky's ear but it took some doing. I set up an appointment with my vet and also my farrier, Barry Spangler, to trim Dinky's hooves. My vet came first and sedated Dinky by injection. I can't remember what he used but he said Dinky would still be able to stand but he would be doped up. Barry came about a half hour later. We had Dinky in the small section of the barn (that you use for training) because it was raining. When Barry opened the Dutch door and came in Dinky cornered him and kicked him three times before Barry could get out. He hadn't even touched Dinky!

Next my vet gave Dinky another injection and waited a few minutes. To be fair to my farrier, we don't think my vet waited long enough to start up again (he had another appointment to go to). Dinky just became more hyper and agitated. They were not able to even do his front feet. I know now, of course, that Dinky doesn't like to be in a tight spot with no way out and he gets really upset when there are two men around him. From bad past experiences no doubt.

I called the trainer back and he started working on Dinky with ropes. He explained that in order to be able to handle Dinky, he would need to surrender to humans. So on it went for a year and a half. Dinky would pull away and run away and hurt every person that came to help the trainer. They were kicked, bitten, rope burned and they never came back. The trainer always had a new person with him. He was able to do Dinky's front feet but barely got one of the backs done.

The trainer started coming by himself and he would always have to resort to tying Dinky up and making him surrender to him before he was able to work on Dinky's feet. The last time I had the trainer here was the day he tied Dinky up and made him jump on two legs for what seemed like a very long time before Dinky finally surrendered. By then Dinky was limping. After the trainer left, Pat and I were practically crying and vowed we would never have him here again. Dinky was lame for three weeks. We never called the trainer again and he never called us to find out why. He knew why.

After you trained Dinky with such patience and knowledge we were finally able to try once again to have Dinky trimmed by our farrier, who was also nice enough to try again. You came the day before and gave Dinky a good workout on his back legs especially. The next day Barry came out. At Barry's suggestion, I gave Dinky a tube of Dormosedan gel [a mild sedative]. We waited 45 minutes while Barry shoed Rowdy who was tied right next to Dinky.

I told Barry to just work slowly and quietly, which he did. He started by rubbing Dinky's face and front shoulder. When he started down Dinky's front right leg Dinky automatically picked up his foot for Barry. The same with the left front. Then Barry started rubbing down Dinky spine toward his back left leg and took more time before touching the bottom of his leg.

Dinky picked up his hoof. Barry didn't grab his leg like farrier's normally do. He just let Dinky's leg lean on his leg.

When he got to the right back leg Dinky kicked once but not at Barry, just to let Barry know he didn't like his leg being touched. I was taking pictures and Pat was watching. I was practically jumping up and down I was so excited. I told Barry that I guessed his wife wouldn't have to pick him up at the hospital after all! He said, "Tom did a great job with Dinky."

And with that it was done. It was a memorable and great day for us. That is when I called you to tell you the great news.

Thanks,

Dianne

That wraps up the Dinky Chronicles. I just want to add that such a difficult project as Dinky proved to be really helpful in my horsemanship journey. By putting me way past my comfort zone, this little mule challenged me to see if I had skills, patience, and knowledge enough to help him.

The experience of working for clients was still new to me then. That brought with it added elements I was unaccustomed to—having an audience and the responsibility of getting a job done in a way that helped the owners continue to work with Dinky to build on the work I did even after I left. Perhaps of most value to me was straight-up seeing my horsemanship put to the test like never before.

The Maddens' farrier, Barry Spangler, finally is able to trim all four of Dinky's feet on October 25th, 2012. *(Dianne Madden)*

I questioned myself plenty during those Dinky Days, but the funny thing was that I didn't really do so during the sessions themselves. I recognized that in the heat of the moment in the paddock while working, I never wondered if what I was doing was right or wrong. The work there was too direct, for lack of a better word. If things got rocky, I switched up my approach immediately and went off in another direction to get a change for the better.

In retrospect, there never seemed to be time to worry while we were working...we just worked on things. I always found a way to get Dinky's thoughts back with me and get him to a better place than when I arrived. It was only later, when I was elsewhere reflecting on various Dinky Days, that I wondered if I was getting things right for him in the big picture.

Dinky showed me conclusively that what I've taken from Harry's teaching, first and foremost, is the basis for all the positive work I do with horses (and mules!). None of Dinky's progress would have been possible at my hands were it not for the years of study with Harry.

Furthermore, Dinky showed me that now when I'm put in a situation with an equine far more troubled and different than anything I've encountered before, I am capable of helping somehow. By using what I've learned from Harry, combined with my own experiences, I can help such a horse or mule get to a better place. Experiencing this through Dinky's dilemmas has increased my confidence many fold.

Lastly, writing these books may be a hopeless obsession of mine, but they also played into the success with Dinky. I discovered as things unfolded at the Maddens' that to write about horsemanship as Harry teaches it, and I experience it, requires fervent focus—the fact that I had clarified many hard to understand aspects of horsemanship through that process on the page really helped me to own and later access that knowledge.

I sincerely hope such knowledge spills over from the writing of these books to the reading of them and helps others to gain clarity into some of my lessons. Also, when sharing with Dianne and Pat as I worked with Dinky, I saw clearly another point the books provided. By spending so much time over the years using the written word to describe Harry's horsemanship and my experiences with, I enjoy an encyclopedia of words, phrases, and stories readily at hand to share many important points with people. I hope this helps folks like Dianne and Pat to grasp ideas that will further them in their ongoing pursuit to better assist the horses and mules in their own lives.

So, thanks again, Harry...and thanks to you too, Dinky!

Tom took this photo of Dinky with his owners, Pat and Dianne Madden, in early January 2013, then Dianne looked over at Tom and said, "Oh my... that's the first time Dinky has let the two of us stand beside him without running off!" *(Tom Moates)*

Afterword

The last chapter shows a triumphant moment in my work with Dinky, and it just wraps things up too perfectly. I felt the need to add just a little here to say that Dinky's hind feet are still a trouble spot that we continue to work on. He has his good days, or perhaps it is that I have days where I better present things to Dinky, so it goes well. But we have the other kind of days, too. I always make the point to get to some kind of good spot with him before quitting for the day. It is so rewarding that the work spills over so he feels better in his regular life, and it helps others handle Dinky in general.

That's the way this horsemanship journey goes—there is profound progress and then the next challenge awaits you there. Getting a horse or mule feeling better about something can be a mystery to be solved which in turn leads to seeing the next level that needs work.

It's like Harry says: "Until you see it, you can't see it; then when you see it, you wonder how you never saw it before." I might add: "And then you're not seeing the next thing…until you see it, and then you wonder how you ever missed that!"

And so on….enjoy the journey!

(Bob Grave)

About the Author

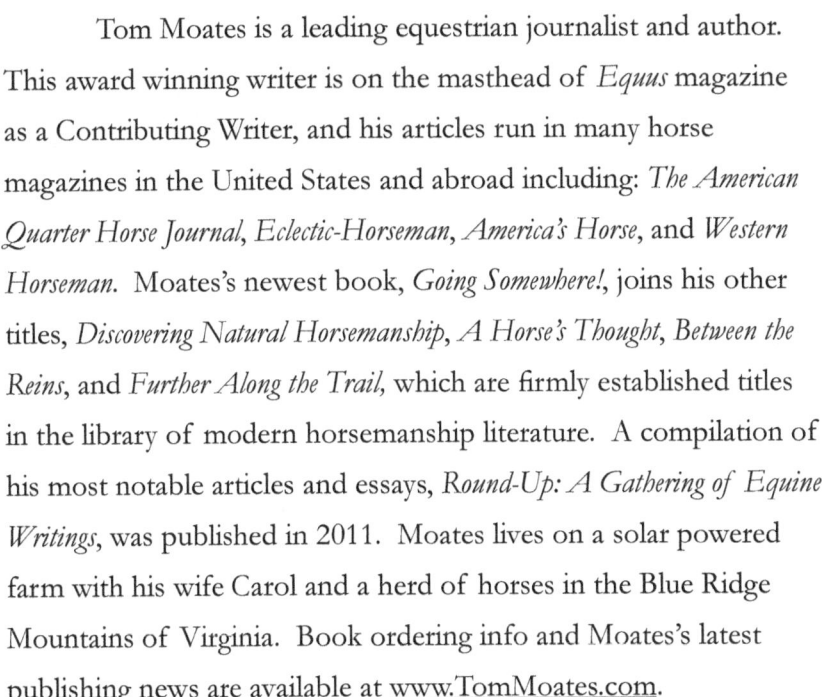

Tom Moates is a leading equestrian journalist and author. This award winning writer is on the masthead of *Equus* magazine as a Contributing Writer, and his articles run in many horse magazines in the United States and abroad including: *The American Quarter Horse Journal*, *Eclectic-Horseman*, *America's Horse*, and *Western Horseman*. Moates's newest book, *Going Somewhere!*, joins his other titles, *Discovering Natural Horsemanship*, *A Horse's Thought*, *Between the Reins*, and *Further Along the Trail*, which are firmly established titles in the library of modern horsemanship literature. A compilation of his most notable articles and essays, *Round-Up: A Gathering of Equine Writings*, was published in 2011. Moates lives on a solar powered farm with his wife Carol and a herd of horses in the Blue Ridge Mountains of Virginia. Book ordering info and Moates's latest publishing news are available at www.TomMoates.com.

www.ingramcontent.com/pod-product-compliance
Lightning Source LLC
Chambersburg PA
CBHW031957080426
42735CB00007B/427